Almost Full Circle

From Montserrat to Canada and Back-ish: A Memoir

JACQUELINE GREER GRAHAM

Almost Full Circle is a work of nonfiction. Some names and details were changed to protect the privacy and identities of the people included.

ISBN: 978-1-7781002-0-8 (paperback)
ISBN: 978-1-7781002-1-5 (eBook)

Published in Canada
Jacqueline Greer Graham
Toronto, Ontario, Canada
jacquelinegreergraham.com

Cover by Bridget Lu. Cover picture by Trinity Design
Structural Editor and Proofreader: Christine Gordon Manley
(Rosemount Writing & Editing Services)
Copyeditor: Adebe DeRango-Adem

Dedication

This book is dedicated to my children, Gabrielle and Lemuel, who inspire me to be my best everyday.

Acknowledgements

Thanks to everyone who shared/validated stories, jogged my memory, and/or provided feedback on early versions of the manuscript (Annette White, Gabrielle Graham, Olivene Dyer, Maxine White, Annemarie White, Alice Brookes, Cecil Bramble, Silford "Nyce" Moore, Venerine Bradshaw, and Brenda Daley).

Thanks to my mother, who is one of the hardest working persons I know, setting an excellent example for me, and all her children.

Thanks to my editors who provided invaluable feedback, guidance, and encouragement. I've learned a lot from you.

Table of Contents

Introduction

Over the years, I've shared many stories with people about growing up in Montserrat, which is Catalan for "jagged or serrated mountains." I've shared countless tales about immigrating to Canada from this small Caribbean territory. Several people told me to write a book, but I didn't appreciate the importance of documenting my story, preserving it for my children to help them navigate life and help others, until the pandemic emerged in 2019. Living through a global crisis gave me a different perspective, as suddenly all our lives were changed: we couldn't do many of the usual activities, like going to the gym, dining out, visiting friends and relatives, or heading to the office. I know people who got sick, and some who passed away. I observed how quickly things can change.

The pandemic continues to impact our economies, health, and well-being. Supply chain issues and labour shortages have impacted the prices and flow of goods across many industries. Businesses continue to experience staffing issues, difficulties converting to a pandemic-friendly model (e.g., online shopping with delivery and/or curbside pickup options). For some, government wage subsidies have proved insufficient—many who lost their jobs or had to accept temporary lay-offs are still unemployed; many people struggle to make ends meet. Healthcare staff and those at essential businesses, continuously exposed to the virus, are experiencing exhaustion and burnout; this is compounded by feelings of underappreciation as a result of a bill that limits compensation increases for many public sector workers, as well as protocols that sometimes put their health at risk; some are walking away from their jobs. Some are working from home and also have to supervize their children's online learning. Reports of domestic violence have increased, as well as opioid-related deaths; health services continue to be impacted due to a backlog of surgical interventions and some are deferring medical help due to fear of exposure. The pandemic has highlighted systemic issues, too. We see how it has disproportionately impacted racialized communities and vulnerable populations such as seniors (especially those in long-term care), the homeless, and BIPOC (Black, Indigenous, and People of Colour) communities.

We said names like George Floyd and Joyce Echaquan, told their stories and cried for them, as if we'd known them all our lives. In the midst of the turmoil, we used innovation to stay afloat and implement solutions. We ramped up our fight against inequities and injustices and pushed for substantive changes in education, healthcare, policing, film, television, performing arts, and more. We wrote books; we created music and art. We took a time of crisis and made it an opportunity for healing, transformation, and restoration.

It's against this backdrop that I reflected on my life. I drew on creativity to cope with the pandemic and wrote this book (my pandemic baby!) to capture my life on a small island and the many years I spent in a big country before attempting to return to my first home—a challenging experience, as it had transformed in catastrophic ways. As with the devastation caused by the pandemic, some things will never be the same, but our ability to innovate, recover, adapt, re-imagine and rebuild, propels us forward to better days.

• • •

My book is based on my memory. I changed some names and details to protect the privacy and identities of the people included.

The story is divided into four parts: as you read Part 1, you'll be transported into my early life in Montserrat, before the Soufrière Hills volcano erupted, and experience my culture, as I navigate both the pleasant and unpleasant situations that shaped my identity. In parts 2 and 3, you'll travel with me to Canada to see how I adjusted to life there, and how I continue to be shaped by my experiences. In Part 4, you'll head back to Montserrat with me, after the volcano erupted.

Writing this book gave me a better understanding of how my experiences and culture shape who I am and has helped me confront some traumatic experiences. It has helped me see the importance of things like kindness, courage, joy, happiness and gratitude—not taking things and people for granted.

As I prepare to publish my book, it has been two years since the pandemic emerged. We continue to experience supply chain issues and labour shortages, contributing to high inflation rates and a rise in the cost of living (food, gas, vehicles, housing). We've seen multiple increases and decreases in the number of cases, hospital admissions and deaths. We are currently in the fifth wave. The fight for equity and justice that intensified during the pandemic continues, and so does the fight over how to handle the pandemic (mask mandates or not, vaccine mandates/passports or not)—implementation varies across provinces/territories. But it also varies across the world because of inequities and mistrust: challenges with access to vaccines, lack of infrastructure like proper fridges for vaccine storage, countries not willing to share vaccine patents so developing countries can manufacture them, lack of trust in governments and scientists, etc.

Overall, Canada and a number of other countries have done relatively well with their vaccination roll out. When variants of the virus emerge in countries with low vaccination uptake, however, we should consider that "their" issues with inequities are our issues as well, for those issues will find their way to our doorsteps, despite travel restrictions, which often come too late. Hopefully, we can get to a point where we have an equitable implementation of vaccines and protocols and can resume normal activities, even if that normal looks new.

I hope this book can bring some joy and inspiration to you, dear reader, as we continue to fight and recover from major events in recent global history. Thank you for taking the time to read it.

Part 1

Montserrat

About Montserrat

Follow me on an imaginary helicopter ride over Montserrat. We'll get a bird's eye view of its three vibrant green mountains—Silver Hills in the north, Centre Hills in the middle, and Soufrière Hills in the south. They lie proudly like giants across its surface. These mountains and the island were formed from volcanoes.

It's the year 2022, so we can see some activity from the Soufrière Hills volcano, which has been active for more than two decades. From our helicopter, we might be able to see Antigua and Barbuda, Saint Kitts and Nevis, and Guadeloupe—the islands nearest to Montserrat. We might also see a small plane or ferry moving in the southwest direction from Antigua, which is about 54 kilometres away. They would have passengers taking the 20-minute flight or hour-and-a-half ferry ride to what is known as the Emerald Isle of the Caribbean.

In Hollywood time travel style, we'll accelerate our flying speed and travel all the way back to 500 BC. We'll now see that this Caribbean gem was inhabited by the Arawaks, and later, the Caribs (Amerindians/Indigenous peoples). They named it Alliouagana—land of the prickly bush. Travelling forward from there to the 1400s, we'll see Christopher Columbus sailing by and hear him naming the island Montserrat, as it reminded him of the Montserrat mountain range in Spain.

Travel forward a couple of centuries and we'll see Montserrat as it was in the 1600s: major upheavals, interruptions, death, destruction, injustices, and other course-changing events. We'll see the English colonizing Montserrat by sending Irish settlers there; some were indentured servants. They laboured on sugar, cotton, and tobacco plantations. Later, we'll see the English arrive with enslaved Africans, who would also labour on the plantations, and eventually become the majority population.

If we had the power to rewrite those events, our story would unfold with cooperation, treaties and fair trade agreements, information sharing, networking, mutually beneficial initiatives, and respect. Indigenous peoples have intimate relationships with the land and its cycles. I wonder if we could have mitigated our current climate crisis if we had considered Indigenous perspectives during industrial revolutions.

Travel forward to July 18, 1995, and we'll now see the Soufrière Hills volcano erupting with catastrophic force, after being dormant for almost 400 years. We'll witness instances of the powerful events that created the island, as well as the devastation to its natural resources, infrastructure, and people. We'll consider how we can do our part to reduce global warming and hold countries responsible for the largest carbon emissions, accountable. While it is natural for volcanoes to erupt as the earth goes through its cycles, it is likely they will erupt more frequently and with greater force due to melting glaciers, rising sea levels, and pressures from big weather systems, like violent storms.

Finally, we'll return to the year 2022, where you'll see that Montserrat's story is far from over, and that in spite of our history,

Montserratians are recovering, adapting, re-imagining and re-building. We'll see that Montserrat is still there, still beautiful with its vibrant green rolling hills and jagged mountains, even though some are scarred from volcanic activity, and that it's still progressing, bringing in new visions for a sustainable future.

For now, buckle up, we're heading to the 1970s…

1 Dreaming of Canada

It's Montserrat in the 70s, where my earliest childhood memories begin. I remember attending nursery school (daycare) in a part of my village called Pond, around three or four. I was a shy child, but my teacher tried to bring me out of my shell, encouraging me to participate in singing and other activities. I felt happy and confident when I enthusiastically sang songs like "If You're Happy and You Know It." I felt less confident when eating at a table and chair that seemed very high; I kept thinking that I'd fall. Otherwise, most of my time at nursery school was uneventful—I tend to remember unusual, dramatic or traumatic experiences; there were many of those, as you'll soon see.

As I grew older, I remember daydreaming a lot about what Caribbeans call "away," or "foreign" (aka "overseas" or "abroad"). In my mind *away* seemed beautiful, and consisted of two places:

Canada and England (sometimes called the mother land/country). Some of my relatives lived in Canada and England, so those were the two countries that I kept hearing about. I didn't know much about them, though.

Did pussy cats really visit the Queen?

Was everything covered with snow?

Was life better there?

I didn't yet appreciate the extent to which England, Canada, and other countries were connected to, and impacted, my little world—British colonialism, Irish settlers, the trans-Atlantic slave trade that brought Africans to Montserrat and other countries, post-slavery exploitation like apprenticeship and sharecropping schemes, resort and residential tourism, immigration, and more. But I had questions, many of them.

My mother, Annette, gave birth to me when she was in her late teens and then immigrated to Canada when I was two-and-a-half. At the time of my birth at Montserrat's Glendon Hospital, she worked at a clinic in Bramble Village as a nurse's assistant, sterilizing equipment, doing urine tests for diabetes, preparing and stocking medication, dressing wounds, and more. It was a job she got after finishing secondary school and completing informal training. Her bigger job, however, was becoming a teenage mother. She wasn't afraid, though, as she thankfully had support from family, friends, and colleagues.

My mother didn't marry my father. I was told that he visited me from time to time when I was born but died when I was young. For most of my childhood, that was all I knew about him. People who didn't know about him would ask, "Jacqueline, where's your father?" And I'd always reply, "dead," in a matter-of-fact way. If someone asked me how he died, I would say, "I don't know and I don't remember him," which would usually end the conversation.

I didn't have any early memories of my mother either, having been so young when she immigrated to Canada. Most Canadian expatriates and seasonal residents (snowbirds) lived in Spanish Point, in the east, near the clinic where my mother worked; most American expatriates lived in the west. My mother had heard from Canadian residents about an opportunity to go to Canada on a domestic visa. It was based on a West Indian Domestic Scheme immigration policy. My mother was able to immigrate a few years after the scheme ended because it continued under a points system. It attracted many people from poor families like mine and was aimed at filling domestic jobs vacated by Canadian women, who had started working outside of the home more after World War II.

So, my mother bravely left her home and family to seek better employment opportunities in Canada. It was a relatively easy transition because she had friends who had already immigrated, and she knew some "snowbirds." She didn't experience the isolation and loneliness that some of the first waves of immigrants experienced; by that time, cultural events like the Caribana Festival (now called The Toronto Caribbean Carnival) had already been established.

When my mother first immigrated to Canada, she worked for a family, doing domestic work—cleaning, childcare, etc. It was a step down from her nurse's assistant job, but she kept her long-term goal in mind, which was to become a nurse. When she began her studies, she quickly realized that she didn't like the blood and guts aspect of nursing. Although she'd dressed wounds when she worked at the clinic in Montserrat, having to dissect pigs made her revisit her career aspirations. She continued to do domestic work and was fortunate to work for employers who treated her relatively well—some of her friends who'd also immigrated to Canada, under the West Indian Domestic Scheme, had negative experiences.

The plan offered mutual benefits, though—it helped Canada meet its labour needs, albeit cheaply, and Canadian families got the help they needed so they could pursue their career aspirations and raise their social status—having help staff does that for some people. The plan also exposed women like my mother to more opportunities, and many found success in manufacturing, education, healthcare, politics, and more. The Honourable Jean Augustine of Grenada became Canada's first Black female federal Cabinet Minister and Member of Parliament. As for my mother, she eventually transitioned to working in a factory, where she worked as a machine operator first, and later, a group leader.

She wasn't the only family member to leave Montserrat. Her maternal uncle and some of her siblings immigrated to England. They were part of what is called the "Windrush generation," named after the ship that carried many immigrants to England. There were opportunities there to fill jobs due to labour shortages after World War II. While the schemes helped fill England's and Canada's labour shortages, they had the opposite effect in Montserrat, where severe labour shortages impacted the economy in devastating ways. Families were impacted, too. Some schemes, like the one from Canada, were geared towards single-person immigration, which separated children from their parents and left them in the care of relatives. In my case, I was left in the care of my grandmother, Esther, whom I called Mama.

When my mother left for Canada, my grandmother and I went to the airport to see her off. As she was leaving to board the plane, I ran after her, crying. I don't have any memories of that but can imagine the separation anxiety that I must have felt. I surely must have been confused about why my mother didn't come back; my mother must have also been emotional, although excited to embark on her journey.

My relatives who immigrated to England also left their children in my grandmother's care. Like her, many Caribbean grandmothers did double/triple duty, raising their children, grandchildren, and even their own elderly parents. Once my mother and other relatives settled in England and Canada, they sponsored their children. I didn't feel sad when my cousins left to be with their parents because my grandmother would tell me often:

"Jacqueline, one day you'll go to see your mother.

She'll send for you."

I would answer, "Yes, Mama."

Now, imagine that you're meeting my grandmother. You'll see a hard-working, extroverted, generous, spiritual, strong negotiator who was a key influencer in my life. She was born in Montserrat, as were her ten children. She didn't marry any of her children's fathers, though—it's possible that none proposed to her. Some of them provided support, but not consistently. Sometimes she had to take them to court to force them to pay child support. Mama didn't play!

I'm not sure how much she was able to work outside of the home with that many children, but one of her first jobs was with the government—pounding stones into gravel. When she started the job, she pounded the wrong kind of stones and was distraught when she didn't get paid. It was very stressful, especially on top of experiencing "baby daddy" drama. Quickly learning from her mistake, she improved her productivity, and the next pay day was a happy day. She eventually transitioned to working at the Bramble Village Clinic as a nurse's assistant. Later, she gave that job to my mother and worked on the land instead. I guess human resources management was still maturing back then.

My grandmother was a tireless guardian to me, as well as to her two youngest children—Cecil and Brenda—and my two cousins, before they immigrated to England to be with their parents. She never told us that she loved us—many Caribbean parents and grandparents didn't express themselves like that. But I was certain that she did, even when she disciplined us. Once, when she was about to lash me, I ran to a neighbour's house. I don't remember what I'd done—maybe I forgot to do a chore—but I came back later, thinking that she'd forgotten about it. I cautiously sat on the front steps, where she was also sitting, and waited for her reaction. Seeing none, I breathed a sigh of relief and naively concluded that disciplining me was no longer a priority. I was jolted back to my senses by the familiar sting of lashes on my back and arms, from a small whip that she'd kept hidden.

Swack, Swack, Swack!

It was too late to run, because it was over before I could lift my weary feet off the ground. Surrender was the only option at that point, but it was also easy to accept my punishment as I never sensed any feelings of anger or ill-will from my grandmother.

Her youngest child, Brenda, was one year older than me, and Cecil was a few years older. I perceived them to be like older siblings, close to my age, so I never called them aunt and uncle. They didn't have any issues with that, back then, but feel differently now. That is understandable, as Caribbean and other cultures have strict rules with regards to honorifics and showing respect. They might say "you too rude!" or "you too disgusting!" if you called your elders or certain relatives by their first name. Out of respect for our culture, I'll refer to Brenda as my aunt/sister. Aunt Brenda was extroverted and funny and liked entertaining people. I was introverted and glad that she was the centre of attention, but sometimes wished I could be as bold as she was. She didn't seem afraid of anyone or anything.

One morning we awoke to the house shaking violently. We thought it was the Concord flying by. When it flew over Montserrat, we felt the vibrations and would run along with it, yelling,

"Cancard a come! Cancard a come!"

"The Concord is coming! The Concord is coming!"

My aunt/sister had already gone outside and came back in to get me. She was excited and wanted me to come out to experience it. Being more cautious, I opted to wait things out inside, while marvelling at her fearless attitude. The shaking soon stopped and we went about our day. We learned later that it was an earthquake—an indication, perhaps, of Soufrière Hills' volcanic activities to come. I don't think anyone was hurt but my aunt/sister had another story to add to her repertoire; others told elaborate tales of the earth opening up and swallowing people. Stories that would have gone something like this:

"Dardy Gad o Lard! Aiuo! Wan man drap na wan hoale dis marnin!"

"Oh God, oh Lord! A man fell into a hole this morning!"

Cecil, although a young man, was strict, and sometimes took on the role of a father figure, so I'll use the uncle (rather than uncle/brother) honorific for him. When Uncle Cecil joined the Montserrat Defence Force, I remember he became even stricter. If he saw me, my cousins and aunt/sister out in our village ("gallivanting," as my grandmother liked to say), he pointed authoritatively in the direction of home. He didn't have to say any words; we knew it meant we'd better get home quickly and before he did, or else we were going to get lashes. Sometimes when he tried to lash us, we ran to Great Grandmother Bertha—I called her Granny. She also lived with us; it was common for elderly parents to live at home rather than in homes for the aged. We hoped that Granny would save us from Cecil's wrath. Although blind and bed-ridden, she tried to protect us.

"Cecil, leave Annette's pickney [child] alone!" she'd bellow.

He ignored her most of the time, but I think our punishment was less severe because of her. She had a kind and warm disposition, and, although I have limited memories of Granny, I was always fond of her. She and her husband had five children, and were themselves likely children of parents who were once enslaved. I can only imagine the treasure trove of stories that are long buried with them.

Granny lived much longer than my great-grandfather, who passed away when my mother was a toddler. However, because of her sight issues, she couldn't do many of the things that she enjoyed, like cooking. It was her children and grandchildren who noticed a change to the great meals that she cooked—sometimes she would use the wrong ingredients. This was when she started losing her sight; she would eventually become completely blind.

My grandmother's boyfriend also lived with us. He was my aunt's/sister's father and she seemed to have a close relationship with him, but I didn't. I wasn't fond of him. I don't recall him ever disciplining me, but he also didn't interact with me. When he came from work, he usually had something nice that he'd brought for my aunt/sister. I don't recall feeling bad that he didn't bring things for me, or jealous of their relationship, or lonely that my parents weren't around. That's probably because my grandmother and great-grandmother filled the role of my mother, and my uncle sometimes filled the role of my father. Besides, I was going to Canada one day to see my mother.

2

The Simple Life

Looking down over the southeast part of Montserrat, you'll see Harris Village. It was previously a plantation/estate, named after the Irish slaveowner who ran it; a common practice for naming plantations. We lived on a hill in the village. From the front of our house, you will see the beautiful Caribbean Sea and the imposing Soufrière Hills right there, in the backdrop. I didn't appreciate their magnificence as a child, though; they were just always there, like pictures on a wall you pass every day and barely notice. We had few material possessions but had everything we needed and some things that we didn't, including rats and snakes—which I definitely noticed. Follow me on an imaginary tour of our property.

Starting at the front of the house, you'll see that it didn't have a lock, and that was likely the case for most front doors in our village; neighbours trusted each other. We'll walk up five or six steps, then through the front door and into the living and dining rooms, both sparsely furnished. You'll see a table and a couple of chairs in the corner of the dining area, on the left. A kerosene lamp graces the table—we didn't have electricity in my early years (so no telephone or television), also common in our village. You wouldn't have heard these words at most houses:

"Somebody, get the phone!" or, "Turn down the TV!"

There were no "couch potatoes" in our house; I remember there being a few chairs in the living area on the right, but I barely remember sitting on them. There was a side table or small cabinet on which were framed pictures of my mother and other relatives. I often looked at the pictures of my mother and dusted them.

When will I go to Canada to see her? I wondered.

When I wrote letters to her, I reminded her to "send for me." There were no pictures of my father, though, and when I asked about him (usually because someone had asked me about him), my grandmother reminded me that he was dead.

To the right of the room is a partition meant to create a separate bedroom, probably for my two cousins and uncle. Many of my mother's siblings and cousins lived in the house, before I was born. Somehow, they made it work in the small space. Further into the house, off the living room, is the doorway to my grandmother's bedroom. There is a bed and some bottles on the floor, near the headboard. I called them lotions and potions, as my grandmother used them to rub us down when we were sick, paint our skin ritualistically, sprinkle some to ward off spirits, and more. To the right is another room about the size of a walk-in closet, with enough room to fit a small bed. This is my great grandmother's room, where she spent most of her latter days. When I tried to avoid getting lashes from my uncle, it was to this room that I ran.

I slept on a sleeping mat on the floor, in my grandmother's bedroom, as I was a bedwetter. In the mornings, I did the walk of shame to hang out the mat to dry on the clothesline and tried to hide the big, jagged, wet circles. When my grandmother couldn't stand the smell, which strangely never seemed to bother me, she used a washing board to hand wash them. Then she let the environmentally friendly lines of clothes dry in the warm sea breeze.

In my younger years, my mother, grandmother, and uncles got water for bathing, washing, and other things from the river, and later from water tanks. We bathed outside and used a latrine (outhouse), as there was no plumbing and therefore no bathroom in our house. At night, we did our business in a chamber pot (aka a "po"). I used to dream that I was using the po, only to be disappointed in the morning when, yet again, my clothes and bedding were soaked. For those times when we used the po, we emptied it in the morning, in the latrine or at the side of the house, depending on the contents.

Throwing pee at the side of the house wasn't a big deal. It was where we sometimes quickly ran to relieve ourselves. The place where my grandmother also administered her special kind of torture—at least that's how it felt to me. She and other proponents of "urine therapy" believed in the therapeutic benefit of drinking urine.

"Jacqueline, drink de pee!" she would say. I was supposed to pee in my hand and drink a couple of sips.

"Mama, mi no like um." [I don't like it."]

"Yu haffo [You have to] drink a little, Jacqueline!" she'd insist, strap in hand.

After futile resistance and tears, I surrendered to the salty, metallic, god-awful taste of liquid waste. Some people still use this strategy, and it's arguable whether it has any health benefit. Having had the dubious honour of knowing how pee tastes, I have a strong preference for drinking fluids before they're converted to waste.

Walking from the side of the house to the back, you'll see the crawl space where we sometimes played. My grandmother's room was right above it. There were holes in the floor, which is probably how rats got into the house. To be fair, they may have been mice, but we called them rats. My uncle or grandmother set rat traps in the night, and in the mornings we saw dead and sometimes live rats in them. Small, non-poisonous snakes may have also come into the house through the holes in the floor; there were a couple of times we found a snake under my grandmother's bed. I don't recall seeing them at night, though; if they ever came on or near us then, I would have slept through that excitement as I'm a deep sleeper. I would later develop a phobia of snakes, but I hadn't yet by this point in my life. I knew I didn't like them, though.

There were no snakes in the new bedroom one of my uncles helped to build. He was a carpenter, so he supervized improvements to the house—a two-storey extension with electricity and plumbing. It included a kitchen on the lower level and a veranda, new bedroom and three-piece bathroom (sink, shower, and toilet) on the top storey. The toilet was a significant improvement over the latrine. My uncle may have installed it around the time when latrines were being replaced by flush toilets in villages in Montserrat. I can't recall how old I was; I also can't remember if we got toilet paper. If so, that would have been an improvement over the leaves that we used sometimes, or the times when we didn't use anything. Regardless, we didn't have to go out to the latrine anymore, and that was fantastic! It was still on the property, though, so if we were desperate, it was an option.

One of the doors in the bathroom was connected to my grandmother's bedroom, but we'll go through the other door from the bathroom to the new bedroom at the front of the house. This was Cecil's new room and the best bedroom. The roof didn't leak like it did sometimes in the older part of the house, and it was vermin-free.

Walk with me through the other door in my uncle's bedroom and we'll head out to the veranda, which I liked, except when it rained, and water collected on one side due to improper slopes for drainage. Sometimes, we had to brush off the water. So be careful where you step as we go through the door off the veranda and back to the living/dining room. We'll go back out of the front door, turn right, and head down to the kitchen on the lower level.

There were a couple of steps to the kitchen door where my grandmother used to sit to eat and do chores. Sometimes, I helped her.

"Jacqueline, bring de coconuts mi a mek [I'm making] sugar ciak [cake]."

"See dem ya [Here they are], Mama."

"Si dung [sit down], come griate [grate] dem [them]."

"Yes, Mama."

Walk up the steps and through the door, and we'll enter the first room. We stored things there but it was probably a dining area without a table and chairs. Sometimes snakes hid under things in this room; they may have come in through the opened door. The cooking area is in the next room, on the left. I remember there being counters, not so much a kitchen sink, and definitely not a stove or fridge. My grandmother salted meats to preserve them. If we needed ice, we got it from a neighbour who owned a fridge. Instead of a stove, we used a coal pit. It was a stone or cement structure that my grandmother filled with charcoal and lit when it was time to cook.

Leaving the kitchen, we'll head out to the yard to see the animals on our property including chickens (aka fowls), goats, and pigs, and we may have had a donkey at one point. The pigs were kept a short distance from the house—house pigs were unheard of. The goats roamed nearby and I had my own goat. We picked a special weed for the goats and pigs, maybe the chickens, too.

"Jacqueline, go pick French weed!" my grandmother would say.

Off I went below the house in a damp, bushy area to pick them. I didn't like that chore, getting my hands dirty in the over-saturated mud. So I would scornfully pull a few weeds out of the ground and come back beaming with pride that I'd done my job. I would watch the disappointment wash over my grandmother's face as she pointed in the direction of the bush.

"Chile, go back and pick more French weed!"

I would take so long to come back sometimes that my aunt/sister would eventually come to my rescue. She had no qualms with picking French weed. She pulled them out aggressively and always came back with a big bundle, to my grandmother's delight.

• • •

We'll take some of the weeds to the chickens in the chicken coop, near the back of the house. My aunt/sister and I helped to feed them and check for eggs. We watched out for the snake in a bottle that sat on top of the chicken coop. My uncle had caught a snake and put it in a bottle, capped the bottle, drilled holes in the cap, and put the bottle on top of the chicken coop. I don't remember if it was meant to scare us or keep other snakes and animals away from the chickens. Regardless, I didn't like seeing it there, slithering in the bottle, its pale underbelly pressed against the glass. Yet, this was not what caused my snake phobia. My uncle never killed the snake and would eventually release it, only to replace it with another one later.

He or my grandmother killed chickens, though. When they cut off the head of a chicken, it would flop across the yard.

"Look, de chickin no [isn't] dead, de chickin no dead!" I said, the first time I saw it.

"E a go dead [it will die] soon," my grandmother explained.

Once it stopped moving, I helped to pluck the feathers out. My uncle also slaughtered pigs and goats, cooked some, and gave some away to relatives and neighbours. None of this was traumatic, even when he slaughtered my goat. It was our way of life.

Heading back towards the kitchen and the front of our yard, you'll see that growing crops was also part of our way of life. We had a couple of mango trees. One of them was grafted by joining branches from another mango tree to its branches. I remember seeing parts of the tree wrapped to hold the grafting in place. When it was mango season, it produced the sweetest mangoes that I'd tasted, similar to July mangoes; grafted or not, I've never tasted a mango that I didn't like. My grandmother and other islanders "genetically engineered" mangoes and other crops before genetic engineering became a common phrase. Evidently, good things can come from mixing/integrating things. We also had coconut, pear (aka avocado), bread fruit, banana, papaya (aka paw-paw), and bread nut trees, as well as dasheens, yams, callaloos, long foot cabbages, peas, sugar canes, tea bushes, and more.

I had a small garden, where my mother enjoyed planting flowers, before she immigrated to Canada. My grandmother allowed me to plant anise seeds and a few other things there; anise and peppermint were my favourite teas. I liked the strong minty flavour of peppermint and sweet licorice taste of anise seed. They were more appealing than the bitter mix of bush teas that my grandmother made from soursop, fever grass and other leaves. The bush teas were supposed to be good for reducing fevers, passing gas, cleansing our gut (aka wash outs), and just about any ailment. I shed many tears when my grandmother brewed her special concoction and insisted that I drink it.

"Jacqueline, drink you tea!"

"Mi no like um [I don't like it], Mama!"

"Chile, drink de ti [the tea], e [it's] good fu yu [for you]."

She also boiled goat milk until the scum formed on the surface. She added cocoa or Milo sometimes, but I didn't like the consistency of the scum and always tried to scrape it off when she wasn't looking. Although my grandmother had a bent towards alternative medicine, she also appreciated traditional medicine. On Clinic Day, she took us to the village clinic to see the nurse and/or doctor, as needed.

If you define "poverty" based on material things, we were poor and so were a lot of people in our village; some would consider us to be suffering from material deprivation, lacking "essential" necessities like a fridge, stove, and TV. But our basic needs for family, community, food, shelter, and healthcare were always met, sometimes in unconventional ways, but that was home. We lived off the land and made the most of what we had. Sometimes you have to use a bucket to catch the rainwater from a leaky hole in the roof, or brush it off the imperfectly sloped veranda, until you can do better.

3

Harris: To Lookout and Beyond

If you've lived in a village, you probably know the sense of community that you get from being in a small, sparsely populated, geographical area, as well as the challenges you may encounter.

I lived relatively close to the Blackburne Airport, located in a village called Trants. It was later renamed W.H. Bramble Airport, after William Henry Bramble, Montserrat's first Chief Minister (role now called Premier), who was in office at the time of my birth. We could travel along the main road from the airport, then through villages like Bethel, towards my village. Instead, we'll walk up the hill north of the airport—in Montserrat, many places were either up or down a steep hill; you wouldn't expect anything less from a volcanic island. I don't think there's an official path there, so as we have to do sometimes in life, we have to create our own. We'll need good hiking shoes and a cutlass to cut through the weeds and kusha/acacia bushes. Kusha has many prickles or thorns. It is probably what Montserrat's Amerindian inhabitants had in mind when they named Montserrat "Alliouagana"—"land of the prickly bush." We used to get pricked sometimes.

"Mama! Mama! Kusha chuke mi na mi [pricked me in my] foot battam!"

"Come chile, leh [let] mi tek um [take it] out."

My grandmother used a big pin or needle to dig the kusha out, while pouring oil on it. But I'd change my mind.

"No Mama! …no tek um out!"

"Chile, stap move!"

It was normal, but pointless to scream and writhe; it had to be removed. After some struggle, finally, it was out—the tiny splinter that caused so much pain!

Try to avoid kusha as we continue.

• • •

A little further up the hill, there were one or two large water tanks that stored our fresh water. We weren't allowed to play there, so we'll only stop to stash the cutlasses and continue up the hill to Barkin. My cousin Olivene lived there with her mother and sisters.

Continuing the climb, we'll get to Cross Road, the only four-way intersection in our village that I recall. We won't turn right, as I didn't visit that area often. We'll turn left, instead, and walk to the top of the hill. You'll see Emmanuel Seventh Day Adventist church on the right. I attended the Harris Methodist church with my family on Sundays, but as the Seventh Day Adventist church's services were held on Saturdays, we also went there for visits. One of our neighbours took my aunt/sister and I there many times.

We'd start off in the main service and after what seemed like a very long time, the service ended, except it didn't. We soon realized that it was a transition break. The children were ushered to another room to continue children's service. We would have said to ourselves,

"Dardy Gad, o Lard, da church ya lang e [this church service is long]!"

After what seemed to be another very long time, children's service ended, and one would think the service had ended...except it didn't. It was another transition break, in which the children were ushered back to the main service. There, we spent another long time. Then it was finally over, and I was bored, hungry, and beyond ready to leave. Still, I was learning tolerance for different religious denominations.

Turning left, we'll continue past a few houses. If we'd turned left again, we'd find the path leading to my maternal grandfather's large house. He was a successful butcher and baker, despite his struggles with alcoholism. Sometimes on the weekends he would be so drunk he would fall down, lying there so long that children would make fun of him by throwing flour on him. I was told that he took care of me in the early days of my childhood but died when I was a toddler; I don't have any memories of him. He didn't marry but had two children with my grandmother (my mother and Uncle Basil) and two children with another woman.

As my grandparents weren't married, my mother was given my grandmother's last name; as my parents weren't married, you would think that I would have gotten my mother's last name but I got my grandfather's last name instead. That's because my mother adopted his last name for use in school. Other people that my mother knew did the same thing. Back then, school administrators didn't have a strict process for documenting personal information; they weren't strict at the hospital either because my mother was allowed to use her father's last name when she registered to deliver me. So, the hospital staff recorded it on my birth certificate. Bob Marley would have probably called this one big "mix-up mix-up!" Data managers and historians probably still get headaches from this practice.

There were some other challenges related to my grandfather. He left informal instructions for his first-born child to get his monetary assets after his death; it was a substantial amount. She was away in England and didn't come back soon enough to claim it. Meanwhile, one of his relatives ensured that his "bastard children" didn't get his money.

In Montserrat and other countries, the illegitimacy law considered me, and others like me, to be illegal/unlawful children—"bastards." In fact, it was written on our birth certificates, which surprised me the first time that I saw it as an adult. It was a jarring label and categorization, but more importantly, it impacted rights with regards to getting our father's last name, support, inheritance (generational wealth), and more. The systems and laws were designed to prevent children like me from succeeding and facilitated poor outcomes, like poverty. They also unfairly impacted women who bore the brunt of the responsibilities for taking care of the little bastards, if you will. I'm glad that many countries revised or abolished their laws—Montserrat, the United Kingdom, Canada, and others—and stopped punishing children for their parents' actions. My grandfather died around the time that illegitimacy laws were changing. I wonder what a difference it would have made if his wealth was passed to my mother and her siblings, in the form of real estate, finances, businesses, or even related knowledge and skills. Maybe we can do things differently for the next generation.

If we continued all the way down the path, we'd end up back at my cousin Olivene's house in Barkin. Instead, we'll continue past more houses and go near the end of the road where my uncle, the carpenter, lived with his wife and children. This area was called Harris Lookout and, in fact, Lookout probably spanned from the Seventh Day Adventist church to the end of the road. It was a fitting name as it was at the top of the hill, and you could look down and out and see the airport, sea, and Spanish Point. You could also see villages that were similar to Harris, like Farms, Bethel, Bramble (where some of my cousins lived), and probably Tuitts and Long Ground. We'll stop for a quick visit at my uncle's house—it was always quick, as he was stern. He loved to discipline his younger siblings, nieces, and nephews in dramatic form. It is likely because his maternal grandfather, my great grandfather (Granny's husband), used to beat him a lot. In fact, that is how Granny's husband died—of a heart attack, while lashing my uncle.

One time, my uncle was at our house and I was running away from him to avoid getting lashes. My other uncle and cousins caught me and held me in the air by my limbs while he lashed me. I don't recall seeing any welts on my skin or feeling terribly upset after getting the lashes, so this experience might be a strong memory only because it was so dramatic. I also don't recall what I'd done wrong, but I took my punishment and went on my way, hoping never to do the thing that inspired that kind of drama, again.

"Good marnin [morning], Uncle. Mama sen dis fu yu [sent this for you]."

"Tell your grandmother, thank you."

"Yes, Uncle."

We usually stood at the door and marvelled at the spacious, neat, and sterile-looking house.

"Goodbye, Uncle!"

As we leave, we'll take in the view from the top of the hill as we inhale the fresh sea air.

"Aaahhh!"

• • •

Continuing down the hill, we'll arrive at the house of a kind neighbour who had a television—the only neighbour who had one, that I recall. One day she invited my aunt/sister and I over to watch a show. It was likely Sesame Street, which first aired in 1969. We huddled around the small television set and waited for the show to start. Finally, there it was—creatures that didn't look real but were talking, singing, dancing, and interacting with each other and with people. I sat wide-eyed, wondering how it was possible that someone had figured out how to make dolls come alive. My friend had told me it was possible if I gave them something to eat. When I tried, they ended up with worms, literally, from the rotting food. Even my grandmother's lotions, potions and rituals couldn't do the job. It would be years before I figured out the Muppets.

Wave goodbye to our neighbour and all the folks from Sesame Street.

Next, we'll head to the house of the neighbour who took us to the Seventh Day Adventist church. We enjoyed treats there sometimes, after attending the long service. No wonder we kept going back!

Just before we go, let's pick a few plums from the black plum tree at the entrance of her property. Be careful, though, as once when I was picking plums, I almost picked a snake out of the tree—the first time I realized that snakes were in trees. Horrified, I dropped the plums and ran away; but this was *still* not when my snake phobia started. Okay, pick some plums and run!

As we continue along the road past a couple of houses, I'll tell you about my experience with a different kind of snake. My grandmother used to send me to a house to run errands. I could easily predict the behaviour of the man who lived there and was very cautious when I interacted with him. He would try to grab and pull me into his house.

One time, I had to go into his kitchen to pick up something. While I was there, he started pulling me into his bedroom. He also started tickling me so that it would seem like a fun game. Then he asked his son, who was close to my age, to help him but it didn't work. I managed to fight them off and run but I suspect that he was using a grooming strategy. He was opportunistic, like a rat, and predatory, like a snake. Creatures like him knew exactly who to target and groom—the shy, quiet child, the one least likely to say anything, and to whom they had easy access. He was right. I didn't tell my grandmother or anyone because I couldn't articulate what was happening.

I've learned that introverts like myself get energy from within. I tend to remain calm in stressful situations and look for a solution, instead of asking for help. I wish I'd told my grandmother, but I'm grateful that I recognized what he was and was able to get away.

If we keep going along the road, we'll pass a few houses and eventually arrive at our house. Instead, we'll turn right and go up the hill to Mrs. Ponde's house, where she lived with her husband. She was a nice lady and one of the few people who had a fridge. It was to her house that we went to get ice.

"Good afternoon, Mrs. Ponde! Mama sen mi fu [sent me for] ice."

We usually had something to give her in exchange; I think we were bartering. Sometimes she had relatives visiting, likely from England, and we would go there to play with the children, in the yard. We'd listen to them tell their stories with melodious accents. They would have inspired some of my dreams about "away."

If we keep going up the hill a few metres, we will arrive back at the Seventh Day Adventist Church. So we'll turn left instead, walk a few metres, then left again down the hill towards our house.

4

Harris: Our House to Mos Ghaut

We lived on a large plot of land. Historically, land ownership in Montserrat was tied to plantations/estates, bought and sold and passed down through generations. Our freed ancestors had challenges buying land due to systemic price barriers—a way for plantation owners to force them to continue to work for them as apprentices ("learning to be free"), and later as sharecroppers.

Based on the surnames included in "Harris" documents I've seen online, some families of our ancestors eventually purchased land in the mid-1800s, including my great-great-grandparents. They would have passed our land down to my family and other relatives, who owned part of it. Some might argue, however, that humans are more stewards, rather than owners, of land.

We'll continue walking down the hill towards our property, then turn right and walk a few metres to our house.

"Mama! Mama!"

I always called out to my grandmother when I came home from school. She was consistently there and always had food prepared.

"Yes child, I'm here. Come eat."

"Yes, Mama." I was a picky eater, though.

"Jacqueline, eat more food! You too skinny!"

I thought I looked perfectly fine; but she thought it was better to be fat—the Caribbean mindset, where being plump was indicative of happiness. She enjoyed food but ironically wasn't a big-bodied woman.

My grandmother also enjoyed Rum Punch, a beverage a number of Caribbean islands produce. Montserrat had its own Rum Punch (Perkins or Perks). If it was my birthday, my grandmother would give me a capful of it. She did so every year, as far back as I can remember, but at no other time. It was exactly one capful—no more or less. It probably contributed to my love for wine, when I got older. That was it—no cake or presents, but I didn't feel deprived; it was normal.

An incident that wasn't normal was a physical altercation between my grandmother and another person in the village. It was about work she was doing on the land. I learned about it when I came home from school and heard her and my uncle discussing it. She had a long, deep cut that extended from mid-leg to above her ankle.

"I cut myself on the iron stake in the ground," she said.

It was a stake at the lower end of our property where we tied animals, sometimes. Her explanation didn't make sense to me. But while it is probably what happened, I was thinking the person with whom she was in the altercation was responsible. I was so upset that I wanted to go to the person's house and give them a piece of my mind, hit them or something. Even though I was shy, my anger emboldened me.

"Mama, I'm going to the person's house."

"Sit your little self down, and stay out of big people's business!" she told me.

With hesitation, I sat my little self down and fumed, worried about her. There's a colonial notion (English proverb) about children being seen and not heard; the idea that children have nothing to contribute because they couldn't possibly understand adult affairs. This impacted the way many Caribbean parents raised their children; it's why my grandmother would have told me to stay out of her business.

She also kept the police out of her business. I don't remember anyone going to them for anything. She simply went on with things with help from us and neighbours. But maybe she would have gone to the police, if I'd told her about my experience with someone she trusted.

• • •

My grandmother sent me to sleep over at a family friend's house after his wife died. I think I was to "keep the daughter company" (stay with her so she wouldn't be too sad). I went to their house and played outside with the daughter; we went inside when it started getting dark. Her father became enraged when he saw me, raising his voice to a shouting level:

"Why is she still here?"

I thought it was strange as it was my grandmother who sent me; I assumed she spoke with him. I'd visited the house many times before, and he'd never gotten upset. I'd never seen him react like that. I kept quiet and tried to process what was happening. We got ready for bed, and I learned from the daughter that I couldn't sleep in her room.

"My father said that you have to sleep on the settee (sofa), Jacqueline."

It was in an open area, like a short, narrow, dark hallway. I went to sleep on the settee and slept soundly through the night, as I usually do. In the morning, as I awoke, I felt there was someone lying beside me and realized it was the father. As I became more fully awake and was trying to get up, I realized that he had one of his fingers in my vagina. I pushed his hand away and climbed over him to get off the settee, where he still seemed to be asleep. I didn't know where my panty was, and I didn't want to stay to look for it, so I went out to the front and opened the door and walked home confused and dazed. Unable to articulate what I'd experienced, I didn't tell anyone. I went to school and put it out of my mind. The next time my grandmother told me that I had to go back, I mustered up the courage to tell her.

"Mama, I don't want to go back there!" But I didn't tell her why.

She insisted that I go, so I went back reluctantly with a horrible feeling in the pit of my stomach. The daughter and I played outside again and, as it was getting dark, she told me to come in the house; once again, her father got upset. This time, he said that I had to stay outside so I waited out there. It was getting dark, and I didn't want to walk home by myself.

Why didn't I just walk home?

I could hear him shouting:

"She's evil! She's bad! I don't want her in here!"

In that moment, I was certain of who I was, even though I was only five or six years old. I remember how old I was because I was in either Standard A or B (junior or senior kindergarten). One day, I didn't wear a panty to school. I didn't think anyone would notice and thought that I was being careful not to expose myself. I wasn't careful enough. As I stood at the top of the Standard A steps, I forgot about my bare bottom. A girl standing at the bottom of the steps noticed that my panty was missing. She started mocking me and telling other children about it. They wanted to see.

"O garm [gosh], Jacqueline no have an no panty!"

Feeling embarrassed, I offered an explanation.

"A wan hoaly hoaly panty." [It's a pant with holes].

Running to the latrine (outhouse) to avoid more mocking, I waited there until the bell rang. When I went back to class, everyone had forgotten about it. The only time that I couldn't find my panty and would have gone to school without one, was after sleeping over at this man's house.

As he continued on his strategic, cruel rant, I continued to wait outside. I felt certain that there wasn't anything wrong with me and that there was something wrong with him. Reverse psychology and projecting weren't part of my vocabulary or knowledge base, then, but I understood, instinctively, what he was doing. I learned many years later that my certainty was routed in facts, that children are very good at sensing manipulation.

Once the shouting stopped, I went inside; he'd disappeared into his room. The daughter told me, once again, that I had to sleep on the settee. I laid down on the settee and, although I was more on guard, I was soon fast asleep.

The next morning, I had the same experience. I only remember those two instances, so those were probably the only two times that my grandmother sent me to sleep over at their house. This man was the biggest rat of the human kind that I encountered. I felt powerless; I didn't have control over the situation. I still get a visceral reaction when I think, talk, or write about this experience, but I'm grateful that it wasn't worse. It made me wise beyond my years. I only wish that I'd told my grandmother about it.

Okay, shake off that incubus and reset with a deep breath... and another.

Now, come and meet some nice people who visited us from "away."

• • •

My aunts and cousins visited from England a few times. I liked the clothes, shoes, toys and food that they brought, and I liked their accents. I felt special when on one visit, one of my aunts styled my hair with a curling iron.

"Jacqueline, my lovely niece, come here, let me style your hair," she said with a distinct British accent, almost singing.

In fact, every time I was in the presence of my aunt, I felt special. I'd seen pressing combs that women heated on burning coals, but not a curling iron. I wondered if the curls were permanent. Time and a little humidity confirmed that they weren't but they were nice while they lasted.

My Uncle Basil, who visited from Canada, dressed nicely and had a swag so I thought he was so cool. I also felt special when I was with him. He brought gifts from my mother and told us that she was doing well and that his wife and son were also doing well. I was too shy to ask him any questions, but I wished that I could go to Canada with him. It wasn't time yet for me to go to see my mother. I would have to continue to wait and dream about "away."

Uncle Basil took us to Vue Pointe Hotel—our first visit to one. He worked there as a bartender, before immigrating to Canada. It was built in 1961 by Michael Osborne, a wealthy, Black Montserratian businessman, and is now owned by his descendants. At six or seven years of age, I hadn't understood the concept of a hotel. Inside of the Vue Pointe Hotel, everything was so fancy, I thought I'd died and gone to heaven. The only other times that I'd seen a few fancy things was when my grandmother opened her trunk—I think most Caribbean grandmothers had one. Her children and other relatives from England and Canada would have sent her the fancy things that she kept in it. It was like the expensive jewellery showcase that you needed the salesperson to unlock. She only opened it for special occasions, like Christmas, and we couldn't touch the things in it. But at Vue Pointe Hotel, I touched everything—the soft sheets on the bed…the plush towels hanging in the bathroom… I'd never seen anything like them.

Wave goodbye to my grandmother and all my relatives from "away," as we head out to the road near our house. Turning right, we'll pass a large plot of land where the owners planted peanuts. Then we'll pass our neighbour's house and another house that was damaged—likely by a hurricane.

Continuing down the hill, we'll descend a flight of stairs to the main road and Mos Ghaut (Mosquito Ghaut), which we pronounced "Mus Gut." It was a gully or ravine that carried rainwater from the mountains to the sea; the main road was built alongside it.

If we turned left and walked down the road, we'd get to the entrance of Bridgefield, where some of my school mates lived. From there, if we continued on the main road, we'd eventually get to the airport. At the Mosquito Ghaut steps, we'll turn right, instead, and head up the road.

5

Harris: Market to Paradise

I walked past the market many times. It was an area off the main road. We would get there by walking from the Mos Ghaut steps, then past Miss Daisy's house; my aunt/sister and I played with Miss Daisy's children, often. There was a short cut through her yard to go to, or from, our house.

Walk with me to the market, past Hammy the butcher, then turn right and walk a few feet to Miss Beebee's Bakery. Miss Beebee's bread was baked in a large, outdoor stone oven and sold in a room beside her house. Enjoy the sweet smell of freshly baked bread as we line up to buy some.

My grandmother used to send me to Miss Beebee's Bakery without any money. While standing in line, I'd rehearse what I was going to say.

"Miss Beebee...I don't have any money, but..."

"Miss Beebee...I need some bread, but I don't have money..."

"Please give me some bread for my grandmother, Miss Beebee..."

Nothing sounded right, so I'd hope that this was the time the earth would open up and swallow me, so I could avoid the interaction. Of course, it didn't, and before long, I was at the front of the line second-guessing whatever words finally came out of my mouth.

"Miss Beebee...Mama sent me for bread, and she said that she'll pay you at the end of the month."

The end of the month was usually when my grandmother received packages, including money from her relatives, from "away." Although my mother and others didn't return to bring their skills back to Montserrat, some of the earnings lost because of their immigration eventually flowed back into the island (aka remittances). Some people did return years later, bringing money and foreign experience back to the island. Back then, though, we were still poor; my grandmother's only other source of income was from selling produce. Maybe some of the money from relatives helped pay for the improvements to the house. I didn't have any of that money, though, so I'd hold my breath and hope that Miss Beebee wouldn't complain about me in front of all her customers. She didn't. She never did, which always surprised me. My grandmother had a credit system, and I guess she paid her debts as Miss Beebee always gave me the bread, without any fuss.

With our freshly baked bread, we'll head back out to the main road. Let's take a moment to sink our teeth into the mouth-watering crust. If you hear me say, "Cheese and bread!" it's not because I want some cheese to go with my bread—it's a colloquial expression of amazement (the equivalent of "Wow!"). Although some cheese would also be nice.

We'll continue to bask in bread heaven as we turn right and

head to the central part of Harris—"out a Harris." I'll call it Harris Centre, for ease of reference.

• • •

This part of our village had a three-road intersection. It was the location of two churches, a rum shop, a spot for vendors, a few shops, and nearby houses. There may have been a couple of other rum shops nearby—many Montserratians love rum, especially on the weekends when people relaxed, drank, played dominoes, and more. Vendors sold roasted peanuts, sugar cakes, and other treats on Fridays and/or Saturdays. The pop-up fish market was another event. Fishermen came by with their buckets full of fresh ballyhoo and gar fish, and people gathered in droves to buy them.

Harris Centre was also a place for entertainment. People stood on a rock, a kind of makeshift platform, to perform. As crowds gathered to enjoy the show, the performer would begin, hoping to be on the rock for a while.

"Brown Girl In The Ring," is a song she might start singing.

Then someone in the audience would say, "I'll pay $1 to keep her up there!" This meant she was doing well.

She would continue singing...

But someone else might say, "I'll pay $5 to take her down!"

I think the next person would have to pay more than $5 to keep her up there. Sometimes audience members would interrupt the performer multiple times, making it hard for them to finish their performance, but this was part of the entertainment.

Continuing on to the left, past the rum shop, is St. George's Anglican Church. The ministers and altar boys there wore extravagant robes, and the services were ceremonial. We visited this church for special occasions like Easter, Palm Sunday, and Ash Wednesday. I remember getting ashes put on my forehead in the pattern of a cross on Ash Wednesday but didn't understand its meaning or that of the other rituals. In visiting this church, as we did with the Seventh Day Adventist Church, we increased tolerance for religious denominations.

Turning left at the Anglican Church and going down the hill, we'll pass the house of my schoolmate with the perfect-looking afro. One of my friends told him that I liked him or his afro. I knew it because one day at school he walked right up to me and said,

"When you have your foolishness, keep it to yourself!"

I couldn't find any words to respond, so I swallowed my embarrassment and kept quiet. To me, it meant that he didn't like me and that I should stop telling people that I liked him or his afro. That was the end of that, or so I thought. I went out of my way to avoid him and comply with his wishes. Then one day, during lunch break, some of us went up the hill behind our school and came back with guavas. He went somewhere else with his friends and came back with mangoes. I could see him walking towards me with beautiful mangoes.

"Here...this one's for you," he said.

I was confused. *Did he want me to keep my foolishness to myself or not?* I took the mango, because I liked mangoes, and said, "Thanks," with very little enthusiasm. Given how rude he was to me before, I decided that I would keep my foolishness to myself. He ramped up his efforts to get my attention, but it didn't work. He continued to bring me things but eventually gave up. Who knew children could be so dramatic?

If we keep going down the road, we'll end up in Bridgefield. Instead, we'll turn right and walk down the street. We'll pass the large graveyard at the front of the Anglican church, and we'll also pass the plum tree. The plums of this tree tasted good but often had worms; no wonder we called them hog plums.

We'll continue and arrive at another business that the butcher owned—Hammy's Shop, where you could get a variety of things. We'll stop in and buy some English sausages, Milo, Ovaltine, and some cheese for our bread. We'll also buy some Dettol, carbolic soap, Bay Rum, Alcolado, and Limacol. My grandmother used Dettol to clean the house, wash clothes, and clean cuts. We used carbolic soap for bathing, which always smelled a little like medicine. Throw on some Bay Rum, Alcolado, and Limacol, to ward off fevers and colds, and we were like walking pharmacies.

If we continue on, veering to the right, we'll eventually find a shortcut leading to my school. Instead, we'll veer to the left as I tell you about another schoolmate.

"Eh, brown skin girl, how you do?" is what he'd say, singing "Brown Skin Girl" to me—a song probably written by Trinidad's King Radio.

I didn't know it was about American World War II soldiers who fathered children with Caribbean women, leaving them in these women's care. I don't know if any of those soldiers came to Montserrat, but we did have lighter-skinned, mixed-looking people, including my schoolmate. In addition to singing to me, he liked to comment on my light skin, in a kind of approving way I didn't fully understand then. I do remember adults and children speaking disparagingly to darker-skinned people, telling them things like, "Move fan dey [get lost], yu black like pat [pot]!"—a slur that, referring to the outside of a pot, typically black from use and unattractive, characterizes darker skin as ugly and less desirable. It's a sad reality that skin lightening creams are popular in the Caribbean and even in places like Canada, albeit more regulated there.

There were other people in our village who were quite fair/clear, likely of Irish descent. Some of them kept to themselves in an "I'm better than you" way—what we called "pretup." I don't recall ever going to their homes or interacting with them to run errands for my grandmother. She was dark-skinned and didn't discuss colour, but she certainly didn't behave as if she was inferior to them or anyone. Other members of my family had varying shades; I don't think I thought about colour. I didn't understand light-skinned privilege in that people may have treated me better solely because of my complexion. My grandmother didn't have any such bias, but Montserrat couldn't escape these tendencies towards colourism or shadism, as a result of years of colonial rule (i.e., the notion that white/fair/clear/light skin is superior).

Continuing on, we'll pass the house of a teacher and another schoolmate, a very outgoing, popular boy who wasn't pretup at all. One day, he asked me to be his girlfriend. Actually, he told me that I was his girlfriend, but our "relationship" didn't last; it was over by the next day.

We'll also pass the Anglican Rectory where the ministers lived, and the sole police station in the village. I don't recall anyone getting arrested. I'd never been near or inside the station but sometimes wondered what was in there. If they had any rats there, like we had at our house; they were probably missing those of the human kind.

• • •

One day, a rat of the human kind visited one of our neighbours while I was playing with my friends. I don't remember how old I was (maybe eight), and I'm not sure where my friends' parents were. The man was in the house in a small room that had steps leading down to the yard, where we were playing. He called out to me in a friendly voice.

"Jacqueline, come and see me. I have something for you."

Naively, I went up the stairs and into the room.

"Sit down, Jacqueline."

I must have already sensed something was off as I sat facing the door, making sure I was still visible to my friends. He sat on the other end of the room, out of sight. He started to show me the food that he had. At the same time, he took out his penis. Quietly and calmly, he said,

"Come and get some food, Jacqueline."

A wave of suffocating discomfort washed over my body, but I didn't panic. I had encountered this creature before and knew what I was dealing with. I sat still, assessing the level of danger that I was in and my next move.

Could I still see my friends? Yes.

Could they still see me? Yes.

I knew instinctively that if I didn't move towards him, he wasn't going to move towards me; he wasn't going to risk being seen. I also didn't make any sudden movements or speak loudly, which would risk getting him angry. In fact, I didn't speak or move at all; I just waited for him to conclude that his plan wasn't going to work. After what felt like an eternity, he realized that I wasn't going to budge so he closed up shop.

"Jacqueline, you can go back outside, now."

He wasn't angry, but he probably thought he'd get another opportunity to try again. After all, paedophiles are methodical and patient with grooming, if necessary. I'm grateful that I had wisdom, gleaned from other unfortunate experiences, to navigate this situation and thwart his plans.

Okay, shake off that rat and let's keep going. We'll walk past the entrance to Garden Hill where we had celebrations (Garden Parties) that the Anglican Church hosted. It is where I drank a lot of goat water, ate a lot of sugar cakes, and drank ginger beer.

Next, we'll go a little further to a house that served as the sole post office in our village; I think this was the post woman's house. She would open the window at the back of the house, which faced the street; sometimes it was a man so maybe her husband or other relative helped too. People gathered above the house and would go to the window to get mail as the post woman called out their name.

"Mr. R. Irish!"

"Yes!" Mr. Irish would push his way through the crowd to get his mail as the post woman called out another name.

"Miss L. Farrell!"

It was very exciting to get mail, which I picked up sometimes. My grandmother got letters and parcels from her children and other relatives. I got letters from my mother. She would tell me that they were all doing well and that I couldn't bore (pierce) my ears or wear halter tops; I used to write to her to complain that Mama wouldn't let me do those things. In my letters to her, I also remembered to thank her for the clothes and shoes that she sent and reminded her to "send for me."

If we continue on the main road, we'll pass the road on the left that would take us to Paradise—where my mother went to get water from the water tank. The government had prioritized installing them for estates, rather than where we and other villagers lived. Later, we got plumbing and the government installed a tank at the market, closer to home. My mother sold green peas (given to her by my grandmother) to the white family who owned Paradise estate, once a sugarcane plantation.

My grandmother and other farmers worked on large plots of rented government land, in Paradise, at the base of the Soufrière Hills. Tourists and locals went there to climb the mountains and enjoy the hot springs, sulfuric landscape, and incredible views, as they marvelled at the jagged wonders. But there was no site-seeing for my grandmother and other farmers. They focused on preparing Paradise's rich soil, using hoes and other tools, with backs bent, heads bowed, and sweat kissing the ground. It was a demanding ritual, like worship.

The end result was a harvest of yams, dasheens, cassavas, sweet potatoes, and other crops. And probably a few physical ailments; it was back-breaking work, and even though she worked so hard, we were still poor. Renting land for agriculture meant my grandmother probably had to spend a good deal of her earnings paying debts. But she never complained and just kept working hard to provide for us. I wish I could say that my aunt/sister and I helped her, but we mostly played between the rows of crops.

We didn't know we were at the base of a dormant volcano that would awaken a few decades later, commanding attention and even more reverence.

6

Harris: St. George's to Blackburne

St. George's Primary School was near the village post office. The Hyde Park Cricket Field and St. George's/Harris Nursery School, where I attended Standard A and B (junior and senior kindergarten), were also nearby. We participated in many activities and events at, and after, school and in the surrounding areas.

One day, my class was in the school yard carving calabashes, a fruit we dried and used to make dishes, decorations, arts and crafts, and more; Montserrat would establish a Calabash Festival many years later. I reached for my calabash and was confused when my schoolmate said,

"No!...dis a mi [this is my] calabash!"

"No!...a mi calabash!" I insisted as we both grabbed it and tussled.

Then I felt the sting of her carving tool. She'd nicked me on the neck—it was a small, surface cut that didn't bleed much.

"Yu cut mi neck!"

"Mi no mean fu [I didn't mean to] cut yu neck!"

I didn't think it was an accident, though. Later, my grandmother took me to the girl's grandmother's house to complain.

"Since your granddaughter can't tell me what happened, I can only consider my granddaughter's account," the girl's grandmother said. "She told me that it was an accident."

My grandmother discussed the matter further with her, and we left.

"Jacqueline, why didn't you speak up?" she asked me on the walk home.

I racked my brain to find an answer.

"I don't know, Mama," I said, feeling like I didn't help at all.

I was fine talking to my schoolmates but couldn't always express myself to adults, especially in stressful or intimidating situations. It was partly because of my natural shy tendency and partly because of attitudes and values reinforced by the belief systems I grew up with, like *children are to be seen and not heard*. There are hierarchical structures ingrained in our culture to ensure children show deference to adults and especially those with authority, like teachers, nurses, doctors, and police officers.

We were taught to show respect, but we were also influenced by the residual impacts of slavery—the painful and sometimes deadly consequences our ancestors experienced when they tried to challenge authorities. This attitude of deference likely made people tolerant to abuse. For me, combined with my shyness, it certainly didn't always serve me well.

Speaking of stressful situations, come with me as I walk home from school, along the side of the cricket field. We'll take a shortcut as we head towards a part of our village called Pond. This is where I remember laughing and chatting and soon running for my life. Come on, run with me! Run! I'll soon tell you why we're running. For now, run with me through Pond as we speed past the houses of some of my schoolmates and the nursery school.

Once outside of Pond, we won't turn right, but if we did, we'd pass the house where a white boy, possibly mixed, lived with his family. This was the only white family in my village that I remember, but there were many in other places—Spanish Point, Richmond Hill, Plymouth, Olveston, Old Towne, etc. Some were Montserratians of Irish and British origin or ancestry, and some had generational wealth from slavery/post slavery exploits and businesses. Others were British, Canadian, and United States snowbirds and expatriates. They were inspired to come because W.H. Bramble initiated a controversial tourism and real estate strategy to rebuild Montserrat's economy; it had taken a hit, starting in the 1950s, as a result of people rejecting and transitioning out of plantation work because of low wages and poor working conditions, as well as emigration to England and Canada.

Bramble, along with the Honourable Robert W. Griffith (a prominent politician), had been instrumental in leading Montserratians to strike against their plantation owners. Bramble went on to become Chief Minister and turned his attention to rebuilding the economy, with resort and residential tourism being a major component of his plan. Tourists could stay in hotels, like Vue Pointe, though they were also encouraged to live on the island. Some purchased highly valued estate land near Blackburne Airport (Spanish Point), Olveston and other parts of Montserrat. As they built their houses and settled, they created some of Montserrat's construction jobs. My uncle, the carpenter, was involved in building the houses. For a brief period of time, my grandmother provided manual laundering services for a white man. My mother's friends also provided maid services. The wealthy benefited by acquiring land and large houses, as well as cleaning and other services (pool, gardening, etc.), and the poor benefited by getting jobs and, in some cases, improving their social mobility. Overall, the Montserrat economy grew, but social inequalities persisted, in that whites continued to fare better—many were part of Montserrat's wealthy class.

There was a middle class that included professionals like nurses, teachers, trades workers, small business owners, etc. My relative, whose mother was a nurse and father a police officer, had a large, beautiful house in another village; I visited them a couple of times. My uncle, the carpenter, my grandfather, and others had nice houses on Harris Lookout and other parts of the village. There were some wealthy Montserratians of African descent; some lived in the same areas as wealthy expatriates. But many, like my family, were poor—an obvious contributing factor being the wealth interruption caused by slavery, and post-slavery systemic barriers, like blocks to land acquisition, lack of education, and unfair labour and agricultural schemes like apprenticeship and sharecropping; they survived by relying on farming and remittances from relatives abroad.

• • •

If we kept going towards Harris Centre, we'd get to the Methodist church, but you wouldn't find any wealthy parishioners there. It was a modest one-room church where I attended services with my grandmother and aunt/sister on Sundays. This was my home church. It wasn't ceremonial like the Anglican church or lively like the Pentecostal church; our services were short, unlike the Seventh Day Adventist church I visited with our neighbour on Saturdays—the one with the long services that left me bored and hungry. At our Methodist Church, we sang hymns like "Christ Arose," gave offerings, and listened to the minister's short message and prayer. Before long, we were outside running around the church yard with our friends. Then we'd walk home with my grandmother.

I liked our church's special events, like Harvest, similar to Canadian or American Thanksgiving. Members brought provisions and other foods to church (coconuts, yams, pumpkins, dasheens, cassavas, breadfruits, breadnuts, sugar canes, bananas—regular, figs, plantains, highty bangela, and more). They would hang the food along the edge of the church ceiling and the side walls and put some on tables at the front. It was as if they transformed the church into a living, breathing, bountiful garden, bursting with colours and scents. Recitals were a big part of the celebrations. One year, I recited a few Bible verses—I memorized passages from psalms and the gospels like nobody's business. I felt proud when people told me how well I did. Then, on the last day of Harvest, we purchased the items and enjoyed food and beverages in the church yard, with all proceeds going to the church.

My grandmother was generous, as Montserratians tend to be, and she involved us in her generosity, like when she sent us to take food to our church's minister. He lived near the Methodist church in Bethel Village, about two miles/three kilometres from Harris. To me, it was far from where we lived (one-hour round trip, at least), especially when I walked by myself. I was fine walking from the Mos Ghaut steps towards Bridgefield, around Sunter Road, and through the populated areas. But once I passed the houses, I had to walk on a long, desolate stretch of road to Bethel. There were bushes on both sides and bulls and cows on one side, and no fence. Sometimes I looked over at them and could see that they were staring at me; I tried to look straight ahead.

I also looked out for a criminal named Joseph or William Fine Twine Bramble, who we heard took children to the mountains. We also heard that he was skinny and could run fast, so it was hard for the police to catch him. It was a true story in the sense that Fine Twine was a notorious criminal on the run, who committed crimes in Montserrat and other islands, but I don't know the details of the crimes. Years later, I learned that in 1974, after searching for him with dogs, the police finally caught him in Montserrat.

What if Fine Twine grabbed me and took me into the bushes?

What if I never saw my family again?

I was relieved to finally arrive at the minister's house. Usually, his wife opened the large doors to their large house. I would give her the food, and she would give me a treat, which made the long walk more bearable.

What was unbearable was having to run; I promised to tell you the reason for our running back there. Two boys from my school had grabbed snakes from the bushes and were chasing us as we headed home. They were laughing, but we didn't share the humour. My feet wouldn't move fast enough as I tried desperately to outrun them.

Keep running with me as we run past Harris Clinic. It was where we went to see the doctor or nurse. The clinic was across the road from the Pentecostal church. We visited it sometimes with friends, enjoyed the lively services and continued to increase religious tolerance.

Veering to the left would probably take us to Cross Road; I didn't go that way often, so we'll keep to the right. We'll run past the upper side of Miss Beebee's house and the Church of God of Prophecy, which was lively like the Pentecostal church. We didn't attend this church but sometimes stood at the door to gawk.

Keep running with me to a large landmark—the Black Mango tree. The mangoes weren't black in colour but sometimes had black spots, which might be how the tree got its name. It was near the house of a man named Brother Reiny, who lived near us.

I walked past Brother Reiny's house many times to go to and from my house. One day, I noticed there was no one in sight at his house, so I decided to stop there to role play, pretending to be a teacher, and banged a stick on the top of the veranda to get my imaginary class's attention. *Bang! Bang! Bang!* I also pretended to administer corporal punishment to one of my imaginary students. *Swack! Swack! Swack!*

Suddenly, Brother Reiny's non-imaginary dog lunged at me, barking angrily. He was sleeping on the porch outside my line of sight. I woke him up with my raucous voice and banging; this dog wasn't happy. Startled and frightened, I ran as fast as I could, but I couldn't outrun the angry dog. He caught up to me and exacted punishment, biting my calf before retreating towards the house at the call of Brother Reiny's voice.

Brother Reiny had a serious disposition and was a little intimidating. I tried to catch my breath and explain what happened. All he said, in a calm matter-of-fact voice, was: "Next time, don't run."

After he checked my calf, I walked home in a daze. My grandmother went to discuss the matter with him while someone attended to my wound. It was the beginning of my fear of dogs, even though we had our own dog named Hero. Hero lived in our yard and wasn't allowed in our house, as was the case with most dogs in the Caribbean.

• • •

But I was running from bullies with snakes, not a dog, so I wasn't about to use the "next time, don't run" strategy. Let's keep running up the hill to Cross Road and then back down the other side of the hill to Barkin. If we would have turned left and headed down the hill, we'd get to the Bugby Hole River. We could go even farther to Fairy Walk and on to Locust Valley, an abandoned estate in the Centre Hills mountains where my uncle and cousins went sometimes to pick mangoes.

Bugby Hole River is the farthest that we'd go, though; we'd wade in the water, catch crayfish, skylark, and lollygag. I wish I could say we went there to swim, but I don't think any of us knew how, even though we had a few rivers and were surrounded by water. On one occasion, I went too far into the deep end and had to stand on the tips of my toes. With some effort, I slowly made my way out. I had done the same thing when I visited Fox's Bay, a popular beach, with relatives visiting from "away." I would have told my young self,

"Stop wading into deep bodies of water until you learn to swim!"

I learned many years later.

Sometimes as we left the river, we relieved ourselves in the bushes ("in na bush"), or behind a rock, using leaves as bum wipes. After running this far from the boys with the snakes, we may have already involuntarily relieved ourselves, several times.

There were snakes on our property, sometimes in our house, and sometimes in trees. But it's different when someone is holding snakes to throw at you. Having experienced this chase multiple times, as I walked home from school, it's probably not a surprise that it is what started my snake phobia.

So we'll keep running. We'll run down the path we created and back to the Blackburne Airport. Here, we can finally stop and catch our breath. Breathe...

7

Let's Go to Town: Plymouth

Plymouth was the bustling and beautiful capital of Montserrat, when I was a child. To get there, we'll travel from the airport, through Trants and Bethel, past the cows and bulls that scared me, and on to Harris. We'll continue past Paradise, on through Farrels, Windy Hill, Streathams, Dyers, Molyneux, Gages, and a few other villages that were similar to Harris; then we'll pass the Glendon Hospital with its beautiful grounds, before arriving in Town.

Town is where my grandmother lost me, one Christmas; or, maybe I lost her. I'll tell you how it happened, soon. First, I'll take you to where I was standing on the steps of a store, when I was seven or eight years old; it was probably on George Street.

My aunt/sister and grandmother were there, too, watching a parade going by. Stand with me and watch the many people wining (dancing), prancing down the street in colourful, often elaborate costumes—peacocks had nothing on them. It was a vibrant jump up and jam session—musicians, perched on trucks, played the sweet sounds of steel pans; other artists joined in, belting out calypso songs. I don't remember cultural figures like John Bull (a person dressed like a bull), Miss Goosie/Goosey (a 12-foot puppet with a wooden frame) or Moko/Moco Jumbie (a person representing a ghost, on stilts), but they may have also been in the parade. Some people danced behind the parade trucks, as they moved with deliberate, snail-like speed down the street. Others, like my family, watched and danced on the side. We'd come to the parade after my grandmother wrapped up business at, or near the Plymouth Public Market—a hub for farmers, fishermen, and other small business vendors.

• • •

I'm not sure when the market closed during the Christmas season, but when my grandmother was at the market, she sold fruits and vegetables at the front stalls. I would watch and listen to her bargain and sell her produce. She was a natural. Everyone seemed to know and like her. She didn't sell everything but never seemed discouraged; maybe she made a profit.

Some vendors sold fresh fish and meat inside the market, and others sold refreshing treats like snow cones outside. Sometimes, my grandmother sent my aunt/sister and I to buy snow cones. Once in a while, we were allowed to go a little farther from the market to buy ice cream. There was also a large toy store not far from Plymouth Public Market, owned by a wealthy white man my mother knew. My grandmother sent or took us to shop there a few times. She also took us banking at the Chase Manhattan

Bank, which always felt very cold—probably from the air conditioner, a foreign concept to me at the time. I also remember going shopping for shoes at Bata. Michael Osborne, the wealthy, Black businessman who built Vue Pointe Hotel, introduced Bata on Montserrat.

One time I ventured into the shoe store by myself. I liked looking at shoes. I was tall for my age with feet to match. I knew this because when I told people how old I was, they would always say that I looked older.

"You're eight? You look like you're ten!" they would say.

Also, the shoes that my mother and other relatives sent were usually too small.

As I was walking through the store, I spotted a $20 bill and picked it up. Back then, for an adult, it was probably like losing $100; for a child like me, it was like finding a fortune. I could feel my heart pounding as I wondered what to do with it. I began to hear a commotion—the person who'd dropped the $20 was desperately looking for it. She had enlisted the help of other people.

"It must be in the store," said a man. Then he pointed to me. "*That* girl is the only person who could have found it. Have you seen it?" he asked me.

"No," I said, fearful of what would happen if I'd said yes. They were so frantic, and he was so intimidating.

My mind raced wildly as I tried to think of a solution. *How do I give it back without telling them that I had it?*

They kept looking around the store, insisting I had it. So I discreetly walked to where I'd found it and quickly ditched it. I casually kept looking at shoes as I moved towards the door so that I could run for it. Then I heard the man say,

"I found it! But I'm pretty sure I looked here already. She must have dropped it here."

I was relieved that they'd found it. But as I quickly left the store, guilty feelings washed over me, as if I'd had gone into the woman's purse and taken her $20. It reminded me of a time when the same amount of money went missing at my relative's house.

• • •

The case of my relative's missing money happened when I slept over at her house one weekend. She owned a liquor store near Wapping, just across the bridge from the Plymouth Public Market and Plymouth Prison. I would first walk there to meet her at the liquor store. Then, I waited in the back with children my age, and sometimes we'd go nearby to pick almonds and other fruit. Once she finished her day, she drove me to her house in Salem, north of Plymouth.

Sometimes, her boyfriend drove us there, if she was drunk; I would worry when she held her head out of the car door to vomit—I was never quite sure if she was alright. On one visit, when she was drunk, she went to bed shortly after we got to her house. I asked a friend nearby to come over to keep my company, and she slept over. The next morning, my relative told me that she was missing $20.

"Jacqueline, have you seen my $20?"

"No, I haven't seen it."

"Are you sure?"

"Yes, I'm sure."

My friend said that she hadn't seen it either. My relative was upset that she couldn't find her money. Her boyfriend threatened to take us to the police station if we didn't give back the $20. Of course, we couldn't give it back because we didn't have it. True to his word, he eventually loaded us into his car and started driving.

"If you don't give back the $20, we're going to the station where there are police and dogs," he warned us again.

Hearing that, my heart rate shot up and refused to settle down. But I was certain that I didn't have the money. I wished I had it so that I could give it back.

"Did you take the money? Why don't you just tell me?"

"I didn't take it! I don't know where it is!" I insisted.

It was as if I was on the makeshift platform in Harris and someone had paid $20 to take me down, except this was going to be much more painful.

As he continued to drive towards the station, I was terrified about what the police dogs and officers would do to us. I didn't want to be bitten by a dog again.

After some time, my relative's boyfriend was satisfied that we didn't have the money. He turned the car around and took us back to the house.

Even at a young age, I was struck by how much alcohol can impact people's lives, as well as those around them and in their care. Not to mention that you might lose money. It influenced my attitude towards (and consumption of) alcohol later in life.

• • •

As we continue to watch the parade go by, my grandmother realizes she has one more thing to do at, or near the market, and will need my aunt's/sister's help. She tells me to wait on the steps of the store, while they disappear into the sea of people in the parade to run the errand.

I wasn't afraid, though. My grandmother had trained me to be independent and self-sufficient. I acquired these skills on the many errands I ran for her. My aunt/sister and I were responsible for dropping off packages, delivering messages, buying or requesting things, and checking to see how someone was doing. We were like packets travelling throughout a computer network—my grandmother's non-digital Harris Village intranet. We learned a lot running those errands.

We ran errands in Plymouth, too, like when I had to take provision food to my maternal granduncle who lived near the

Glendon Hospital. He was a big, tall, strict man with a serious disposition—fitting characteristics, as he was the warden of the Plymouth Prison. When I knocked on the door to his house, I held my breath in anticipation of his deep, loud, intimidating, stuttering voice, piercing through my soul.

"What are you doing here?" he'd ask, as if he suspected me of a crime.

"Mama sent this for you, Uncle," I replied sheepishly, handing him the package.

"Alright...Well, come in then."

That was the last thing I wanted to do. His house was small, dark, sparsely furnished, and fully uninviting. I didn't think saying no was an option, though—my usual attitude of deference to authority.

Before I knew it, I had walked in (or some unexplainable force had pulled me in), and I was sitting on an old chair. My granduncle would start rummaging around, looking for things, sometimes in complete silence. Sometimes he asked me questions.

"How you doing in school?"

"Good, Uncle."

"How you grandmother doing?"

"Good, Uncle."

I'd continue to sit in awkward silence, waiting to be dismissed. At long last he would hand me something and say,

"Thanks for coming. Give this to your grandmother."

If it was close to the time for him to go to work, he would take me to the prison with him, which was near the Plymouth Public Market. As he opened its large, heavy, outer doors, he would say, "Come inside, Jacqueline," his imposing presence filling the courtyard. I would walk in cautiously. It wasn't a place that I liked to go. There were staff and prisoners as we entered, and everyone moved out of his way—like the red sea parting before us. I wonder if his strategy was to show me prison life, so I'd never end up there. If so, it worked.

• • •

What wasn't working for me, though, was the fact that my grandmother was taking so long to come back to get me. I was starting to worry, waiting for her on the steps of the store. The sea of people kept moving down the street. At least I could distract myself by admiring all the elaborate costumes and dancing/wining.

I don't think the "anti-man" was there, but he would have also been a welcomed distraction. "Anti-man" was our crude and inaccurate way of referring to a man who was flamboyant and wore clothes that matched his personality, with a walk more feminine than that of many of the women at the market. People laughed with him and commented on his outfits and hairstyles, but I never sensed that anyone laughed at him. RuPaul, the famous drag queen, told Oprah that when he first dressed in drag, he got an amazing reaction from men, women, and even dogs passing by in the streets. He also famously said, "We're all born naked and the rest is drag."

The anti-man was the closest representation of a drag queen I'd seen growing up, although there may have been others. I liked that he had the courage to show up authentically, and people seemed to love him. It was probably because he was genuine and, on some level, they may have recognized that they, too, had on their own form of drag, per RuPaul's assertion.

So, there were no drag queens or kings in the parade passing by but probably a Calypso King (now called Calypso Monarch, to be more inclusive) and a Carnival/Festival Queen. They would have won calypso singing and beauty competitions that year.

• • •

As the parade of dancing people moved down the street and the calypso played on, I came to the terrifying conclusion: my grandmother had forgotten about me! She'd been gone for such a long time. Naturally, I started thinking of solutions.

One: keep waiting (do nothing)

Two: find my way home (solve the problem)

Three: ask someone if they'd seen my grandmother (get help)

I knew where people waited for buses and taxis and where the person who drives to my village was usually parked, so I opted for solution two—find my way home. I didn't have any money though and probably wished that I had the $20 from the Bata Shoe store or the one that went missing at my relative's house.

• • •

I'd never seen my grandmother drunk like my relative, and I'd only seen her drinking Rum Punch. I knew she hadn't fallen down drunk somewhere. But after waiting for so long, I was convinced that something was wrong, so it was time to solve the problem. Follow me to the taxi area and we'll head home.

"Are you going to Harris?" I asked the driver.

"Yes."

"I think my grandmother forgot to come back for me, so I have to go home."

Climb into the car with me and let's go! It was packed like sardines, and I think I sat on a woman's lap. It wasn't safe, but that was our way of life. After a number of stops, we'll arrive at the Mos Ghaut steps.

"My grandmother will pay you when she sees you," I sheepishly told the driver. She'd trained me well to buy goods and services on credit.

You'll see darkness greet me as I quickly and nervously climb the Mos Ghaut steps and continue up the hill to my house. I didn't see any lights. Opening the door, I called out for my grandmother, aunt/sister, and uncle but no one answered. Sadly, my great-grandmother had passed away a couple of years earlier from old age. My aunt's/sister's father had also passed away, but I don't remember the cause. No one was there. I already knew that, but was hoping that I was wrong.

I waited at home as my shoulders and knees likely touched, creating the perfect ball. Thankfully, I didn't have to come up with creative tactics to ward off intruders, like Kevin did in *Home Alone.*

• • •

There was a nice family friend near Plymouth, whom we trusted, but I didn't think to first go to his house when I lost sight of my grandmother in Town. My aunt/sister and I spent weekends there a few times. I'm not sure if he had a family, but he was usually alone. We slept in a bedroom with two beds; it was nice to have our own beds. Sometimes he gave us gifts; I remember getting a nice doll, albeit a white doll—there were no Black dolls that looked like me back then. One time, I spent the weekend at the family friend's house, without my aunt/sister, but I wasn't afraid. He was always kind to me, so I trusted him. I had the bedroom to myself and two beds, to boot. Crawling into one of them, I curled up and got ready to sink into a nice, deep sleep. The family friend was also preparing for bed and had gone to the shower. He stopped in to say,

"Good night, Jacqueline!"

"Good night!"

He laid down on the other bed as he continued to chat with me. I thought it was unusual that he had a towel wrapped around his waist. As he laid on the bed, face up, he eventually took the towel off and, in a matter-of-fact tone of voice, he asked,

"Can you powder me, Jacqueline?" as if it was a perfectly normal thing for me to do.

I started bawling and kept bawling and bawled some more. Seeing how upset I was, he covered himself and said,

"So, if I was sick, you wouldn't take care of me?"

I kept bawling. He soon left, and I eventually fell asleep. Once again, I couldn't articulate the pattern that I was seeing: projection, manipulation, gaslighting. He was another big rat of the human kind, pretending to be nice all along; I stopped trusting him. When he showed me who he was, I believed him, as Doctor Maya Angelou advised Oprah to do with regards to a different kind of relationship. I'm grateful that he didn't try to hurt me again. I also like that I knew instinctively how to adjust my flight, fight, and freeze tactics to fit the situation.

• • •

My tactic for waiting alone at home was to hunker down and be patient. Keep waiting with me. Soon we'll hear voices finally pierce the deafening silence: my grandmother and aunt/sister!

It felt like I'd been holding my breath all that time and could finally exhale. I ran towards the door. My face lit up and worries faded as I saw them walking up the yard. The scowl on my grandmother's face betrayed her unhappiness, but she also seemed relieved to see me.

"Jacqueline! Why didn't you wait for me? I told you to wait for me!" she said, scoldingly.

"I thought you forgot about me," I lamented. "You took so long to come back. I took a taxi home and told the man that you'll pay him."

"I was so worried. Don't do that again Jacqueline!"

"Yes, Mama," I replied, glad she only scolded me (no lashes this time). Soon, I was sound asleep—likely dreaming about getting up to pee; it's highly unlikely that I did.

8

Come Celebrate With Me

One evening in November, in the yard with my aunt/sister, I remember the sky being clear, but the stars pale in comparison to the big, bright lights in the distance. The whole village seemed to be on fire as people burned tires and pulled them down the road. My uncle and cousins headed out with their flambeaus, made from bottles partially filled with kerosene oil.

Most Commonwealth countries were on fire. They lit up in November to celebrate Guy Fawkes Day/Bonfire Night. For me, and other Montserratians, it was Star Light Night. I didn't know that it was related to Guy Fawkes, who tried to assassinate England's King James the First using explosives in the 1600s. Guy Fawkes and people who plotted with him were arrested. Since then, we celebrate the thwarted assassination every year on November 5. My aunt/sister and I celebrated in the yard, with mini fireworks (star lights), likely purchased from Hammy's Shop. There were many fires during the celebration but, thankfully, no one burned down the village.

• • •

After kicking things off in an explosive way, we got ready for Christmas Festival, which began in December and ended in January. It was a time for parades (like the one we went to in Plymouth), shows, competitions, dancing, eating, drinking, and partying. People made black cake (rum cake), black pudding (blood sausage), sorrel (a beverage made from the sorrel fruit), ginger beer, sugar cakes, plate tart (made with coconut), duckna or ducana (made with sweet potatoes and coconut), and more.

They also made goat water, Montserrat's national dish, similar to Irish stew. As we sit on the steps, you'll smell the sweet aroma of goat water, as my grandmother cooked.

"Jacqueline, come get you goat water!" she'd say.

"Coming, Mama!"

"Chile, stap de coming and come!"

My grandmother had no patience for "Caribbean or Island time." It was what children used sometimes when they were too busy playing. Adults used it when they were busy liming/relaxing or gallivanting, or wanted their own flexible standard for timeliness. It was especially used in non-academic or non-professional settings, although it probably crept into those settings from time to time. "I'm coming" (mi a come) was our noncommittal response that had no urgency/no rush. Other islands might say "soon come." The time you actually come, however, can range from minutes to hours, or longer, and sometimes the person didn't come at all. So, my grandmother's response was both a warning for us to stop wasting her time and a way to set us straight.

I would quickly stop the coming and come. Then I'd fill my mouth and warm my belly with the hot, tasty stew. She didn't have to tell me to eat more; there wasn't a drop left in the bowl when I was done ("Mi niam arl a um!"). Enjoy some goat water with me as I tell you more.

• • •

In addition to celebrating with foods and other libations, Masquerades were a big part of Festival. In *Festival at Fifty 1962–2012*, Montserrat's historian, Sir Howard A. Fergus, wrote about the history and uniqueness of Montserrat's Masquerades. The Montserrat National Trust, and others have also written about them. The custom originated from the harvest celebrations of the Yoruba people in Nigeria, West Africa, and continue in the Caribbean.

As we sit on the steps, imagine Masquerades coming up the path to our yard. They'd immediately change the mood of the evening for me. Before they arrived, I'd be relaxing in stupendous bliss, as my internal processes did their work on my belly full of goat water. But seeing them made my body stiffen and put me on high alert. They were men dressed in colourful clothing, with feminine elements, like lace; this type of clothing was likely a way for our freed ancestors to mock our house/domestic ancestors and house mistresses, when they went from house to house to announce the news about emancipation. After emancipation, Masquerades continued to perform from house to house and at events, paying homage to our West African ancestors.

They would inch closer to our house with their intricate dance steps (quadrilles, heel and toe, Irish jig, improvised steps, etc.) and the rhythmic sounds of drums and fifes—it might as well have been sirens sounding loudly, as I could feel my heart beating out of my chest! I tried to stay well back, but it would beat louder and faster, reminding me of a time when I performed at Sturge Park, where Masquerades also performed.

• • •

Sturge Park was a public cricket field, with a stage for celebrations and a stand for spectators. Famous Montserratian batsman Jim Allen, from Harris, played cricket there, but I don't remember him. I learned that it was named after Joseph Sturge, a wealthy, white British abolitionist who came to Montserrat in the 1800s to champion the fair treatment of our freed ancestors. He helped ensure the end of the apprenticeship scheme, a system which was supposed to help our ancestors adjust to being free but, in fact, forced them to continue to work for their former masters under quasi-slavery conditions—harsh treatment, extremely low wages, and so forth.

Sturge also did other business in Montserrat. He bought land there, and his family and their company went on to purchase even more land—in Olveston, Woodlands, and other areas. They probably could have bought the whole island, if it had been for sale. They did rent and sell some of their land to locals, and even to the government. They established profitable lime and cotton estates that benefited the island as well. So they were rich but also generous and forward thinking. They eventually gifted the land for Sturge Park to the Montserrat government—"The gift was self-rewarding," according to Fergus, in *Gallery Montserrat: Some Prominent People in Our History.*

• • •

I only remember performing at Sturge Park once, during Carnival, which was a big part of Festival; it was after reluctantly accepting the terms of a teacher's ultimatum:

"Jacqueline, you can't do track and field if you don't participate in Carnival."

"Yes, teacher." I liked track and field, so I surrendered to the pressure.

I was the letter T in a group of students whose costumes were also letters of the alphabet. We shuffled on to the Sturge Park stage in a line, and, one by one, each of us moved forward to do a dance. After I did my dance, I couldn't find the spot where I was previously standing. I panicked and quickly rejoined the line somewhere past the middle; the letters were no longer in order. I felt embarrassed about my mistake, but my teacher didn't say anything about it; nor did anyone else, to my relief. Maybe they were amused or didn't even notice that I'd messed up. It was more significant to me than to them, in the grand scheme of things. So I put it out of my mind and enjoyed the rest of the celebrations. I likely tried to avoid getting too close to the Masquerades.

I didn't know the Masquerades' dance was a celebration of our ancestors, though, who danced to connect and communicate with each other. They also danced to mock their masters, by mimicing how they celebrated at parties. It was a way to protest because they weren't allowed to practice their customs: playing drums, dancing, spiritual rituals, etc. They blended African and European customs and used creativity and spirituality to manage their immeasurable pain.

• • •

Another one of our ancestors' coping tactics was singing the original form of calypso, which has West African roots. They put hidden messages in their songs to communicate with each other and entertain themselves. Calypso was a big part of our Festivals with its messages on topics like politics, social issues, gossip, and more. I often memorized and sang calypso songs including a type of calypso called Benna. It was a genre that typically included scandalous content. My grandmother would often say, "Girl, stap singing dem [them] Benna songs!"

Before the Masquerades came to our yard, you might have heard me belting out Trinidad's Slinger "Mighty Sparrow" Francisco's song about a man named Mr. Warner, who had a daughter named Marie. I thought it was about a woman named Marie Warner and that the chorus was "Marie Warner" repeated four times. I learned many years later that it was "marijuana"—a clever use of double entendre.

Montserrat's William "Mighty Ruler" Murrain (Farrell) sang a calypso song in 1974 about Joseph Fine Twine Bramble—the criminal on the run, whom I was afraid of seeing walking to Bethel. I sang the song often—maybe it helped me cope with my Fine Twine fears. You may have also heard me singing reggae songs like "Fattie Bum Bum" by Jamaica's Carl Malcolm. It showcased the Caribbean attitude that having some extra fat is positive.

I don't remember the songs that I sang by Montserrat's Alphonsus "Mighty Arrow" Cassell as a child, though years later I would enjoy singing and dancing to "Tiney Winey" and "Hot, Hot, Hot," two of his very popular songs.

• • •

Masquerades who came to our house didn't sing, but I wished I could stop them from dancing their way up the path to our yard and house. I could see that their masks hid and distorted their faces. They were decorated to mimic the faces of fair or white-skinned people. There was a hat attached to the mask that was similar to the mitres that Saint Patrick of Ireland and other church bishops wore. It didn't give me any warm feelings but our ancestors must have experienced some joy from mimicing bishops. In

1985, Saint Patrick's Day became a public holiday in Montserrat, as it is in Ireland and Newfoundland, Canada. In Montserrat, it is a week-long celebration of our Irish and West African heritage and our ancestors' fight for freedom, when they planned a rebellion on March 17, 1768. They didn't succeed because someone leaked the plan; consequently, their masters executed some of them, and imprisoned or banished others.

The Masquerades' whip was the worst. *Swack! Swack! Swack!* I didn't know it symbolized the tool that slave masters used to brutally punish and control our enslaved ancestors. It was also supposed to communicate instructions to the dancers, chase away evil spirits and simulate lashing the masters. When the Masquerade leader cracked the whip, it felt like it pierced through my flesh, into my soul, and back out. It reminded me of getting lashes, but worse.

They would dance and prance and crack that whip in our yard for what felt like an eternity. My family would drop money on the ground for them as I bawled and hid and bawled some more. Then at long last, they would move on to the next house, leaving me with sweet relief. I appreciated them much more as I got older, though; I appreciated the passing on of our ancestors' dynamic cultural customs, and strategies for managing incomprehensible circumstances.

Serenaders/carolers also came to our house to sing Christmas songs, which was a more pleasant experience and custom for me. I don't recall a big emphasis on Santa Claus; I'd only heard he visited houses and left gifts. So, there were a couple of times when I left socks out to hold them. I went to bed with great anticipation and woke up with the same, hoping to find something—anything—in my socks. But I never did—there was no doll, toy, book, or plane ticket to Canada to see my mother, and my grandmother didn't offer any explanation. When I finally asked her,

"Mama, why doesn't Santa come to our house?"

She broke it to me gently.

"Jacqueline, Santa isn't real."

I imagine that her space was already crowded with fantastic beliefs tied to our ancestors. Plus, with her practical, no-nonsense approach to solving her problems, Santa didn't stand a chance in her world. If he could have brought water from the Bugby Hole River, worked the land (aka grung/ground), or left some money to help pay her debts to Miss Beebee and others, then we'd be in business. So, she didn't think twice about putting my expectations back in line with reality. It was one of the few times in my childhood that I remember feeling disappointed.

9

Have You Ever Seen a Jumbie?

"Jacqueline, your grandmother died!"

A neighbour greeted me with this devastating news one day, as I was heading home from school and walking past the market.

"Mama died? How?"

"I don't know."

It didn't make sense. When I'd left home for school, she was fine.

I hurried home but couldn't get there fast enough. When I was finally closer to the house, I was relieved to see my grandmother alive and well.

"Mama!" I called out to her, catching my breath.

"Someone...told me that you died."

"No child, not me. It's your Granny."

This was how I learned of my great grandmother's death. I felt sad to hear Granny died but it was a little easier to accept than Mama dying, as she was my primary caregiver. Bolting into the house, I ran to Granny's room to see her. She was in a fetal position with her eyes open. I wasn't alarmed, though. She didn't look scary to me, I wanted to know more.

"Why is she lying like that? Why are her eyes open?"

"She was dead for a while before anyone noticed, so she stiffened up."

Rigor mortis had set in, which lasts 36 to 48 hours before it starts to loosen. During that time, no one could straighten her legs or close her eyes.

You'll see that my grandmother prepared Granny's body for burial in the house; Montserrat didn't have a funeral home yet. My uncle helped to put her in a casket but couldn't close it. Her legs were still bent and eyes still open when my aunts arrived from England. My mother couldn't come for Granny's funeral, though, so I would continue to look forward to when she'd "send for me."

My aunts from England were upset when they saw Granny, but someone came up with a plan: "Put bricks on her knees to straighten them."

"Keep checking her eyes to make sure ants and flies don't get in them," another one said.

The aunts reached consensus and, before long, Granny had bricks on her knees and we all helped to keep insects at bay. After some time, her knees relaxed enough so they could close her casket. It was the first time that I experienced someone dying in our house and how hands-on my family was with the deceased—preparing the body, preparing for the funeral, doing whatever needed to be done. None of it was traumatic for me, although I did experience something I didn't like.

Before heading to the funeral service, we gathered around

the casket. Without warning, you'll see that someone lifted me up and quickly passed me over Granny's casket. I ended up in the waiting arms of a relative on the other side. It was unexpected and startling, but someone later explained that it was to prevent Granny from coming back to visit me—one of the rituals related to funerals and jumbies (ghosts/Jack-o-lanterns/duppies) my family practised. I thought about Granny often after the funeral, but she didn't come back; maybe the casket ritual worked. The ritual must have worked for other Montserratians, too, as I learned years later that many of them lifted children over caskets. But I'll tell you about how I heard about my aunt's/sister's father's death and my less pleasant experience…

• • •

One morning my aunt/sister came into my uncle's room, where I was sleeping—it was available when he was away, likely working with the Montserrat Defence Force. My aunt/sister told me her father had fallen down in the living room—and didn't get up. He was dead.

"Come Jacqueline, mi fada [my father's] dead, mi a go [I'm going to] show yu mi fada," she said.

"No sah [sir]!" I replied.

I wasn't fond of him; that was one dead person that I didn't want to see. My grandmother and others prepared his body in the house and put him in a casket. Then came the ritual of lifting the children over the casket. I protested in my head, but also didn't want him to come back to haunt me. I was conflicted. Soon, I felt my body go up and over to the other side of the casket. Once again, I didn't like the ritual but at least I wouldn't be a magnet for the deceased.

• • •

Sometime after my aunt's/sister's father's funeral, I was asleep in my uncle's room, on the floor. My grandmother was asleep on my uncle's bed, and I don't remember where my aunt/sister was sleeping. When I turned, I saw a shadow on the wall that looked like the top half of a man. He was wearing a cap and his waistline ended at the floor. It looked like my aunt's/sister's father, who wore a cap when he was alive. I wondered, *Was it him? They lifted me over his casket so he shouldn't be haunting me, right? Is it dependent on whether you're fond of the person?*

Lying motionless on the floor, I held my breath, closed my eyes, and hoped the shadow would be gone when I opened them again. Then, my grandmother got up and reached for one of the bottles of lotions and potions that she kept at the side of her bed. She started sprinkling things to rebuke the dead, which is how she told the deceased to go away.

"Jacqueline, go back to sleep, everything's alright," she said, having noticed I was awake. *Had she seen the shadow, too?* I wondered. I was too frightened to talk to her about it, but when Mama told me everything's alright, I believed her.

This was my only encounter with a jumbie. It felt like a real experience but it's arguable whether it was a figment of my imagination or a nightmare. On the other hand, my grandmother seemed to see jumbies often. She would rebuke them, sometimes saying "I just saw your Granny," or "I just saw your grandfather," or another deceased relative. She didn't tell us about jumbies or jumbie stories to scare us, but other people did, especially at night.

One of my relatives told us that they saw a deceased person as they walked home in the dark in an outfit that the deceased person used to wear, calling out to them; they kept walking. Another relative told us he'd seen his deceased father before, in the form of a dog.

"He was guiding me home in the dark," he said.

"How did you know?" someone asked.

"He kept showing up every few feet. When I put my foot on a water tank and leaned over to drink water, he put his foot there, too."

"What did you do?"

"I took my foot down, and he took his foot down, too. He followed me all the way home."

I'm no jumbie expert, but unless that dog was transparent or able to defy gravity, or dare I say a shadowy figure, my guess is that it was a real dog, not a jumbie. The story was scary nonetheless.

After hearing these and other stories, I was afraid to go to bed. I'm sure I didn't get up to pee on those nights. The stories could have been worse, like the ones about jumbies throwing things, touching you, preventing you from breathing, or blocking your path. Speaking of touching—you'll notice a well-set plate at the dining room table. Do not touch it! I'll explain what it is.

It was Christmas time, possibly Christmas Eve, when my grandmother went to her trunk, where she kept the fancy things that her children brought her from England or Canada, including the good ceramic plates—the best China, the plates you used for guests. She also got the good tablecloth.

While we ate our dinner on ordinary enamelware plates, my grandmother prepared a single plate for a guest and put it on one side of the table, out of the way. She placed the food on the good plate in a systematic manner, and with the utmost care. I remember how she shaped the rice or cornmeal in a near perfect half sphere, as if she had used a specific number of grains, and how she placed the meat and trimmings perfectly around the rice.

Everything was ready but the guest still hadn't arrived—they were late but my grandmother wasn't concerned. *Who was she expecting this time?* I wondered.

She didn't tell us when we asked. It didn't make sense to me—why they'd lift us over caskets to prevent jumbies from coming back to haunt us, then set a table with the most delicious-looking meal expecting the deceased to come back.

We waited to see if our guest would come and eat the food, secretly hoping they wouldn't show up. We went to bed, and in the morning, we checked the table—the food was still there, in perfect form. I don't know how my grandmother kept the rats away, but even they didn't dare touch it. She may have put a cover on it before she went to bed. Every time we walked past the table, we kept checking the food. It seemed to dare us to touch it, but we didn't—we couldn't. We weren't mischievous enough to eat any, then pretend it was a jumbie. But no one else ate it either. Maybe the guest was supposed to count, but not eat, the rice, as I heard some people say. Or maybe the guest couldn't find their way back and ended up at the wrong house. After all, we weren't the only ones who practised this ritual—many other Montserratians prepared meals for their ancestors to connect with and honour them. What if they all showed up? Wouldn't that be something? Eventually, the plate was mysteriously removed from the table, ending the temptation and anxiety.

In addition to casket rituals, jumbie stories and jumbie plates/tables, some people practised the jumbie dance ritual. It has similar steps as the Masquerade dance and was supposed to help break obeah spells or help people recover from illnesses. I learned that our enslaved ancestors brought the obeah rituals from West Africa. They practised it by connecting with the ancestors to get help with curing illnesses, preventing or resolving bad situations, and influencing people. In "Obeah Wedding" song, the Mighty Sparrow mocks a woman's futile attempt to "work obeah" to force him to marry her, and alludes to his more powerful ancestor. Although there was no organized African church in our village, obeah and the jumbie dance may have been the closest representation of our ancestors' spiritual and religious practises. I don't think my grandmother practised them; I didn't know anyone who did and there was probably a lot of variation in how obeah was practised. However, sometimes my grandmother would express concern about people "working obeah" on her or her family, so she was careful about what information she shared.

10

Your Father's Dead

Walk with me to Mos Ghaut, and we'll stand at the side of the main road, below Miss Daisy's house. Standing there, we're guaranteed to see the cars coming from the airport, filled with visitors from "away." Most were passing through, en route to Plymouth and other places; some were visitors to our village. They came bearing gifts and tales of lands far away.

On a fateful day, when I was eight years old, I was standing on the side of the road, waving at passing cars. My aunt/sister and I, and others, had done this many times. Sometimes cars honked and people waved at us to say good afternoon—that's the most that ever happened.

• • •

That day, as I waved at cars, one of them stopped. It felt like my heart also stopped…or started beating faster, or something—it was doing something different.

I wanted to run, but my legs wouldn't move. Standing frozen, I waited for the consequences of my foolish behaviour as a man came out of the car. He walked towards me, as if floating. I watched him anxiously. I didn't recognize him and had never seen him before, but he seemed to know me. He was smiling, which made him seem friendly.

*Maybe he wanted to ask me a question, or maybe he was on his way to Miss Daisy's house...*I processed the different scenarios as the man continued to float towards me. Then, before I could have another thought, I felt my body leave the ground.

I was now also floating and couldn't breathe. The man had picked me up, and it felt like he was squeezing the life out of me. *Who was he? Why wasn't my mouth working?* Not that it was surprising. My mouth didn't work when I was uncomfortable or anxious—that deference to authority struck again. I was close to Miss Daisy's house and relatively close to home, so maybe I was high enough in the air for someone to see what was happening. *Was it Fine Twine? Was he going to take me away?*

A deep voice finally interrupted my thoughts:

"Hello...I'm your father."

Some people never meet their biological father; some have Luke Skywalker experiences, or meet them in other ways. Ideally, your father introduces himself to you when you're born (or before) and is present thereafter. My father was dead. My grandmother told me this many times, and it was my automatic response when people asked me about him. I didn't know when or how he died, but I knew he was dead. Of this I was certain.

Why would someone lie about my father being alive? It was like a Luke Skywalker/Darth Vader moment, minus the scary mask, deep breathing, and epic lightsaber battle. But, I found my voice, or a sound came from my body that seemed to be my voice.

"No...you're not my father. My father is dead," I said with rare confidence.

My grandmother and other relatives had told me this so many times, there was no question in my mind that what he was saying was wrong.

"I'm not dead," he chuckled. "I'm your father. If you don't believe me, let's ask your grandmother."

I slowly floated back to earth as he put me down, but he didn't let go. Follow me, and you'll see that he kept holding my hand as we walked to my house. I thought it was strange that he wouldn't let go of my hand. As we got closer to the house, I called out to my grandmother, with certainty.

"Mama!"

I was sure this stranger was mistaken and that my grandmother was going to set him straight.

"Mama! Mama! This man says he's my father."

My grandmother looked up at the man and didn't seem surprised.

"Yes," she said, with a look of disdain, and great displeasure in her voice. "That's your father."

That's not what I expected to hear. *How could this be my father? How is he now alive?* My certainty (which was obviously based on false information) faded and confusion flooded my mind. *Why did my grandmother look at him as if she wished he really was dead?*

She didn't offer an explanation; there were other thoughts crowding my mind. I didn't feel happy. I was confused and uncomfortable, mostly uncomfortable.

The person whom I thought was dead was, in fact, alive and my grandmother didn't seem to like him. That was obvious. The reason I felt uncomfortable was less obvious to me and likely to them, and to you, too. My father, who was essentially like a stranger, showed me a lot of affection. He held my hand and wouldn't stop holding me. I wasn't certain he was bad; all the things that I'd experienced to date with rats of the human kind had made me want to pull my hand away. I tried to move away at times, but he wouldn't let me go. He kept holding my hand, hugging me, and pulling me closer to him.

• • •

For the next couple of years, my father "tortured" me with his touches and affection. He would pick me up from school, and it was usually before the end of the school day so he would have to negotiate with my Standard 3 teacher. It was a little embarrassing and felt like I was doing something wrong. He had other children (Silford, Venerine, and Mavis) in Salem (the same village where my relative, who lost her $20, lived). He would take me there to spend time with them. He was divorced from their mother but had a white girlfriend, who also lived in Salem. He would take me to visit her, too, as well as some of his friends. They were all nice, and everyone seemed to like him. In fact, he was a popular tour bus driver. He took tourists around in his Island Tours bus, on which he proudly displayed his nickname, "Nice." His given name was James, but most people called him Nice or by his other nickname, Bratcha—a colloquial way of saying his last name.

My father's girlfriend had a spacious house that was sparsely but nicely furnished. There were some fancy things there that I tried not to touch. She had a German Shepherd, which I didn't like because of my fear of dogs, but also because he was the biggest and most intimidating dog that I'd met. She didn't have any children or toys, so I was happy when my siblings came by to take me out to play. One day, as I headed out with them for a walk, my father warned us:

"Make sure you don't go to the beach."

We went to the beach. When I got back, I couldn't figure out how he knew I'd disobeyed him—maybe the sand on my clothes and shoes betrayed me. It was the first time I remember making my father unhappy. He scolded me and sent me to my room for a few minutes. It felt as bad and possibly worse than lashes.

A more pleasant memory was when I went to a restaurant for the first time with my father and his girlfriend. There weren't any international fast-food restaurants like McDonald's or Burger King in Montserrat. So instead of quickly getting a Happy Meal, I was at a fancy restaurant looking at a fancy menu, for the first time.

"Jacqueline, you can have anything you want," my father told me.

He eventually ordered for me (probably chicken), as it was a little dark and I couldn't see the menu well. After we ate, we spent the weekend at his girlfriend's house. I still didn't like her dog, so I didn't go near him, but he didn't hurt me. So far, my father hadn't hurt me either, but I was still unsure about his character and intentions. He seemed nice, but I didn't really know him. I could tell that my grandmother really didn't like him as she barely spoke to him (and never spoke about him), so I didn't ask her any questions. She didn't even ask me about my visits with him, so I didn't offer any information, either.

I also didn't know if he was back in my life for good. My approach was to take in one visit at a time, and perhaps my grandmother would also take a wait-and-see approach.

11
Skipping Standards

At St. Georges Primary School when the headmaster rang the bell, we lined up in the courtyard for assembly, which could sometimes be dramatic. We formed horizontal lines by class: students in Standard 1 stood at the front and Standard 7 students were at the back. Line up with me, and you'll see us singing the British national anthem, then reciting the Lord's Prayer. At this point, any students showing up late would have to stand at the side. They were the indicators that assembly was going to be a show.

It was as if the headmaster had the lead role, the late students had supporting roles, the teachers and other students were the audience, and the strap was the prop. I was sometimes on the side, waiting to play a supporting role. Then I'd hear the headmaster say authoritatively:

"Greer, Come to the front!"

It was show time! I took my place.

Masterfully, he liked to call us by our last names. It struck fear into my soul, and I imagine that it helped him depersonalize the experience.

Swack! Swack! Swack!

I knew the script, if you will. It was usually three or four quick hits, which I would accept, grudgingly, as embarrassment washed over my face.

I tried to avoid being late, by managing my dilly-dallying ways, so that I wouldn't be in the assembly show; it didn't always work. I walked slowly and moved slowly, in general, as I was a dreamer. I would analyze the flowers, trees, crappos (large toads)—either live or as roadkill—lizards, birds, even people, as I walked to school. If I wasted too much time, I suffered the consequences. Some people walked to school barefoot, mostly by choice, but I preferred to wear shoes, which meant I couldn't attribute my slowness to lack of shoes. I walked so slow that sometimes my older cousin would catch up to me, grab my neck, and push me towards school.

"Hurry up! Walk faster!" he'd say. But he didn't want to be late either, so he'd eventually leave me to my dreaming.

As I, and other children who were late, waited on the side, some put their exercise book under their shirt, in the back. It was their strategy for lessening the impact of the strap. But for the headmaster, it was like an unacceptable prop. It made a distinct sound, so when he heard it, he demanded they remove it; punishment was even more lashes. Some students danced around to avoid lashes, but it was a deviation from the script, so that didn't end well either. Some went home with welts on their skin from the strap. I remember at least one mother coming to complain (likely from a middle-class family). I don't remember if I ever had welts, but my grandmother never complained, nor did most parents. In fact, children were likely to hide their welts to avoid getting more lashes at home.

I've learned corporal punishment had colonial, not African, origins. The colonial influence was likely rooted in a scripture from the Bible:

"He who spares the rod hates his son, but he who loves him disciplines him diligently." (Proverbs 13:24)

It's what some people that I know call the "spare the rod, spoil the child" approach to discipline. Some think the rod is a physical tool for hitting. It could be a pot, pan, spoon, belt, shoe, broom—anything within an adult's reach that children learn to duck and dodge. Others interpret the rod as a symbolic tool for guiding, training, or teaching, like shepherds who used a rod to guide sheep back to the fold. Colonizers, and particularly the churches in Montserrat, responsible for educating our freed ancestors likely embraced the literal interpretation of the rod, implementing corporal punishment in the education systems on the island and the other colonies. Plus, they already had confirmation of the effectiveness of physical punishment in controlling the behaviour of our enslaved ancestors. As students, we didn't like it, but it was normal for us—we didn't know any other way.

• • •

After assembly we went (in order) to our classes. Imagine that you're with me in class. You'll see my teacher meting out more lashes while teaching lessons—continuing the assembly show. I don't recall getting lashes from my Standard 1, 2, or 3 teachers—they were nice, especially my Standard 3 teacher. She mingled with us sometimes during recess. She would even play netball in the courtyard, a sport similar to basketball. My Standard 4 teacher was very strict, though. I don't remember my father negotiating with her for me to leave school early, so even he was probably afraid of her. In her class, I got lashes for not fully memorizing multiplication tables, not correctly completing work on the chalkboard, and more. When she sent a student to the board, it was the suspenseful (cliff hanger) part of the show.

"Jacqueline, go to the board and complete the arithmetic problem!"

I would stand there, frozen, while my classmates (the audience), waited to see the outcome. *Will Jacqueline complete the problem correctly? Or will she buckle under pressure?*

Swack! Swack! Swack!

I felt the sting of my teacher's strap, ending the suspense. I wasn't a drama queen, so I didn't dance around to avoid it, as some students did. Although my face was usually flushed with embarrassment, I don't remember crying. I composed myself, then returned to my seat in the audience. We'd all wait to see which lucky student would be standing at the board in the next scene, if you will. But I still hadn't any idea how to do the problem, so my classmates would have to tune in next class to get their lingering questions answered. *Will Jacqueline be at the board again? Will she finally learn the lesson? Will she cry this time or will she do the board dance?* It was drama that I could do without.

I didn't like the drama, and I didn't know if I liked arithmetic, but I did enjoy reading. We had many opportunities to select books from our bookcase and read during class. *Brer Rabbit, Anansi, The Three Billy Goats, Chicken Little,* and *Who Will Bell the Cat* were some of my favourites. Our village didn't have a bricks-and-mortar library, but we had a mobile library in a big truck that came to Harris Centre from time to time. I enjoyed borrowing, reading, and returning books to this library when it came around.

Looking back, I wish our books and curriculum included more about our history. I remember learning about the Arawak and Carib people, indigenous to the Caribbean and South America. I recall learning that Christopher Columbus "discovered" the West Indies. But I don't remember learning about the history of our

West African ancestors before, during, and after slavery. Nor did I learn the historic and cultural significance of some of our customs and celebrations—the history of Masquerades, the West African origins of calypso, patois/Montserrat Creole (our dialect), and the concept of tricksters like Anansi and Brer Rabbit, who used their cunningness to outsmart their opponents. I didn't even notice that none of our books had Black people. Sadly, it was normal to read books like *Snow White*, *Little Red Riding Hood*, *Jack and the Beanstalk*, and other tales with solely white characters—once again, colonialism at work. I don't know if Black Montserratians were making policy decisions about education curricula; if they were, they were likely plagued with attitudes of deference towards white culture and people. Also, we probably didn't have many Black authors writing our stories; Montserrat would later establish the Alliouagana Festival of the Word (Literary Festival), showcasing local, regional, and international authors.

Some countries have revised curricula to include more of our history and more Black authors are emerging. These changes will help students and others become better local and global citizens—help prevent the repetition of racist practises and systems. Although our books didn't capture all of our history and stories back then, it was exciting when we got new books, and fun delving into them.

• • •

I also loved recess—time for netball, hopscotch, jump rope, marbles, jacks, and other games with friends. I also liked lining up to get a glass of milk—part of the government's health/social program. It was nice and sweet, likely made with Klim (powdered milk).

One day, my Standard 4 teacher approached me during recess.

"Jacqueline, come with me."

"Yes, teacher."

Follow me as we go with her to the mysterious and intriguing teacher's lounge. I'd never been inside but imagined that it had fancy food, beverages, and furniture. We walked past it many times. When the door was ajar, we'd slow down to try to get a good look but didn't see much.

Why did she want to speak to me? I wondered, feeling concerned. She'd never pulled me aside like that. If she wanted to scold me for something, give me lashes, or demand that I do something, she'd do so in front of everyone. One time, she made me wash my face.

"Jacqueline, go outside and wash that powder off your face!" she demanded sternly.

"I don't have powder on my face," I said, as politely as possible, to avoid making her angrier.

She pointed her finger to where the tap/pipe was and repeated herself.

"Go and wash that powder off your face, now!"

I knew that if she had to say it again, it wasn't going to be good. I left the classroom and washed my face. Actually, I rinsed it because I didn't have soap. I was embarrassed that everyone heard I'd tried to wear powder to class. But I hadn't. I don't recall my grandmother wearing face powder, so I'm pretty sure that I didn't have access to any. When I went back to class with my freshly rinsed face, she seemed satisfied that the powder was gone; perhaps the water removed some dirt and oil and gave it a different look.

But that encounter was weeks ago. *Did she think I'd put powder on my face again?* I wondered once more, feeling even more concerned.

In the teacher's lounge, you'll see me standing anxiously, waiting to hear about my transgression. I wasn't thinking about what was in the room; my focus was on what was to come. Then,

I heard strange words coming from my teacher's mouth. First, she told me my mark; I think it was the fourth highest mark in the class. Then she said,

"Jacqueline, you and three other students will go to Standard 7 in September, instead of Standard 5."

Silence.

"You are going to skip two standards!"

More silence.

I don't know which emotion was stronger—relief and happiness to learn I wasn't going to get the mother of all lashes or confusion about what it meant to skip.

Our system allowed students like me to skip standards if our marks showed we had the potential to do more challenging work; I don't think it assessed whether we were emotionally prepared for the change, though—ready to hang with the big children. If you achieved success in Standard 7, you could go on to Secondary School in Plymouth and from there, college in Montserrat or even "away" overseas to institutions like University of the West Indies in Jamaica.

I'd never skipped standards and didn't know anyone who had. I knew students who repeated them, though. One year they were in a higher standard than me because they were older; the next year we were in the same standard.

"Please tell your grandmother when you go home," she continued, breaking the awkward silence, as she ushered me back out of the lounge.

"Yes, teacher."

Walking out in a daze, I wondered: *What will Standard 7 be like with the headmaster, who was the teacher?* He was stricter and more intimidating than my Standard 4 teacher. I didn't know if he liked me or anyone.

Later, you'll see that when I shared the news with my grandmother, she was very happy.

“You’re a smart girl, Jacqueline! You’re a smart girl,” she told me.

I didn’t feel smart, but my grandmother thought I was smart, so I believed her. I imagine she also shared the news with my mother the next time she wrote to her. I don’t know if she told my father (probably not!); I don’t remember telling him. It would be a few months before I’d have to worry about starting Standard 7, though, so I put it out of my mind, as children can do so well.

12

Learning About Away

1977 was quite the year for me. I'd received the news about skipping standards, and, later that year, I noticed that things were rather unusual. For weeks, there was a flurry of activities that involved us getting our pictures taken and going to government offices in Plymouth. I listened to my grandmother talking to a stern, though nicely dressed white man; I didn't understand what they were saying, but I knew things weren't going well. We had to see him multiple times.

"Why doesn't this man want to help me?" my grandmother would ask in frustration, as we left the building.

In spite of her complaints, things worked out in the end. After many meetings, preparations, and much paperwork, my grandmother had some news: we were going to England! It wasn't Canada, but it was "away," and at ten years old, it was my first time going anywhere outside Montserrat. I barely slept as the day got closer.

My grandmother had told us only one or two days before our travel date, and we weren't allowed to share the news. She didn't want anyone to "work obeah" and prevent us from going—that would have resulted in much weeping and wailing. Even though she didn't practice obeah, she seemed to hold strong beliefs in its power. Not even my father knew I was going to England.

I was still getting to know him and going on regular visits to Salem. But I didn't learn until years later why people thought he was dead.

"Jacqueline, I had moved to Antigua where a radio announcer broadcasted that I was crushed by a car that I was repairing."

"Oh."

"The news spread quickly in Montserrat, but it was about someone who either had the same name or a similar name as mine."

"Oh…"

"I was alive and well and was surprised that some people—like your grandmother—thought I was dead."

"Dad, why didn't my grandmother like you, though?" I asked.

"I don't know, Jacqueline."

I'm sure that he didn't meet her standards for consistency and reliability, among other things. But despite her dislike for my father, I was glad I happened to be on the side of the road waving as he was driving by. I was glad that he recognized me.

"Jacqueline, your face didn't change. It was still the same as it was when I left Montserrat," he told me.

Most importantly, I was glad that after getting to know him for a couple of years, I could confirm he wasn't a rat of the human kind! He was affectionate in a way that I hadn't experienced. I liked him and was adjusting to his style; I was adjusting to having a father. But just as we were getting our relationship back on track, he was about to be surprised and upset that my grandmother kept him in the dark about our visit to England. He would have to hear all about it when I returned.

• • •

Come with me as we begin our journey at Blackburne Airport (now called W.H. Bramble Airport). My grandmother, aunt/sister and I had been there a few times, to either welcome or send off visiting relatives. We watched with excitement as they waved and climbed up the narrow steps of the "big" Leeward Islands Air Transport (LIAT) airplane (about 38 or 48 seats). Once inside, they continued to wave from the small windows. We would wave vigorously but were never sure where they were sitting. Then we'd watch with wide eyes as the plane slowly taxied down the runway, turned, sped back down the runway, and, with even wider eyes and mouths, we'd watch it lift off—then, they were gone away, until next time. It always felt like a special event. Sometimes I wished that I could go "away" with them. This time, it was finally our turn to climb the steps and wave, but I barely remember the plane taxiing down the runway or the take off.

Soon, we were at Antigua's Coolidge International Airport (now called V.C. Bird International Airport after the first Antiguan prime minister, Sir Vere Cornwall Bird). It is where we boarded a connecting plane, after visiting with relatives there. In fact, anyone coming to and from Montserrat had to go through Antigua, as Montserrat's airport was too small to provide international access to jets and other big planes. From Antigua, we flew to England, where I didn't see a bridge falling down or a cat visiting the Queen, or snow, for that matter, as it was August 1977. But I did see my relatives who had immigrated there.

• • •

At London's Heathrow Airport, you'll see my aunt and one of my cousins there to greet us. Then we brought our luggage into a large rectangular box. After the door closed, it bounced like the scale the nurse used to weigh us at the Harris Clinic. I looked up to the top and watched as the numbers increased. *How much did we all weigh and why did they need to weigh us?* I wondered. *Did we have too many things?*

The numbers stopped increasing and the doors opened; we came out where we entered, or so I thought. No one recorded the weight, like the nurse usually did, after weighing us. No one said anything to us. So, I concluded that we weren't overweight. It wasn't until much later when we visited one of my aunt's friends, who lived in a flat (apartment), that I learned what it was. At the flat, we went into a rectangular box, similar to the one at the airport. I was confused about why they needed to weigh us again, but was too shy to ask. Eventually, I learned by listening to conversations, that it was a lift (elevator), not a scale. Montserrat didn't have high-rise buildings; I'd never seen an elevator before.

The buildings and lights in England were nice and very different from those in Montserrat. I admired them as we drove to my aunt's house, where we met other relatives. There was a lot of food, and the house was abuzz with activities. Our schedule was so busy, I'm not sure when we slept. We learned and experienced some unusual things when we visited relatives—you'll see one of them introduce my aunt/sister and I to salt and vinegar crisps (potato chips). I'd never seen or eaten crisps or tasted vinegar. I didn't like how it looked or smelled. With a lot of coaxing, I reluctantly put a crisp in my mouth, and—*oh, oh, oh, oh, oh!* It was the most disgusting "food" that I'd ever tasted, by far. It was not like anything that we had in Montserrat. I spat it out on a napkin and simultaneously provided entertainment for my relatives—a role that usually belonged to my aunt/sister. They encouraged me to try it again.

"You'll get used to the taste," my aunt reassured me.

I tried it again at another event and had the same reaction. It still tasted awful.

We experienced another unpleasantry when my aunt's husband decided to treat the boils on our knees. They were infections, likely caused when bacteria entered cuts on our skin. Maybe we weren't consistent with using carbolic soap and Dettol. I was so used to boils I didn't even realize that I had them. You'll see my aunt's husband put me on a chair and start squeezing the puss out, violently.

"Jacqueline, this is going to help you."

The rest of my family, "the audience," cheered him on; I was in tears. Finally, the "torture" ended and he applied the ointment.

Trying salt and vinegar crisps and getting boils treated happened early in our visit. It was as if we'd completed rites of passage—a ritual cleansing and food initiation—and earned the right to enjoy the rest of the visit. We certainly had a great time. My aunt took us to many cool places—Buckingham Palace (to see the Queen, but she wasn't there), 10 Downing Street (to see the prime minister, but he wasn't there, either), London Bridge (completely intact), Kensington Market, Wrigley's Market, Harrod's, and more. The sights, smells, and sounds were otherworldly. "Away" was surpassing my expectations.

Looking back, I realize that I longed to experience life outside my small bubble, whether it was going to see how other people lived or learning from those who visited us. Being in England, I experienced new things and expanded my worldview, even though I didn't fully realize it at the time. I loved the architecture, double decker buses, going to the markets, and buying things with a different currency. I loved fish and chips, the English accent, and the wonderful smell of Palmolive soap (much nicer than carbolic soap). I loved learning about the royal family and the prime minister. I loved all of it.

• • •

But one of my cousins, who I saw bawling her eyes out, had other things to teach me about "away." She was clearly quite upset about something. It was as if someone had died. I mustered up the courage to ask her what was wrong and learned that indeed, someone had died.

"Elvis died," she told me, through her tears.

She seemed to expect me to know who he was. She used his first name only, so I suspected he was a relative I hadn't yet met. I was eager to learn more about him and wracked my brain trying to think of who he might be, but I had no idea. We had visited other relatives but hadn't heard about anyone named Elvis.

"Who's Elvis?" I finally asked, sheepishly.

"Don't you know Elvis Presley?" she asked incredulously.

"No," I admitted, embarrassed. *I knew it. I should've known who he was.* "Who's Elvis Presley?" I asked, expecting her to finally enlighten me about our relative.

"He was a great singer in America, and he was very popular," she explained.

I was confused. More questions swirled in my head. *Where was America? Why was Elvis popular? How did he die, and, most importantly, why was my cousin crying as if she knew or was related to him?*

"I've never met him, but you can see him on the tele (television)," she added.

She was right—he was on the tele a lot. People were talking about him and playing his music.

In Montserrat, I hadn't met any celebrities; not that Montserratians fawned over them. Unless you were the Queen or a member of the royal family, you could visit and blend in. You'd be greeted by friendly people but wouldn't have to worry about paparazzi or obsessed fans.

Famous musicians like Stevie Wonder, Sir Elton John, Sir Paul McCartney, The Rolling Stones, and Sheena Easton wouldn't visit to record music until 1979—when Sir George Martin (The Beatles' producer) opened AIR Studios Montserrat. I also hadn't met the Mighty Arrow, the Mighty Sparrow, or even the Mighty Ruler yet. Learning about Elvis Presley was my introduction to popular culture and the phenomenon of the celebrity or "rock star." I wouldn't appreciate, until many years later, the significance of the death of the King of Rock and Roll.

In that moment, I was fascinated by the fact that my cousin bawled for a man to whom she wasn't related and had never met. I had this and so many stories to tell my friends and family back in Montserrat about "away." But I returned a few weeks after the school year started, and had to face painful consequences.

• • •

I don't know why I, along with my grandmother and aunt/sister, returned so late, but my teacher, the headmaster, wasn't happy about it. I found it difficult to catch up and understand some of the lessons, and it wasn't in my teacher's nature to pamper students. I was just going to have to figure things out.

In one class, he showed us how to do a math problem on the board. Then it was our turn to try one.

"Greer! Go to the board and solve the problem!" he said, with such authority that every thought floating anchorless in my head ran away, if you will, farther than Forrest Gump did when he ran across the United States, trying to understand his life. I should have run away with them. Instead, I went to the board and stood there, frozen, waiting for the inevitable—the familiar sting of lashes across my back.

Swack! Swack! Swack!

As I did when I got lashes from my Standard 4 teacher, I was always left to wonder: *How will this help me find the answer?*

I kept failing tests but hid my marks from my grandmother.

As far as she was concerned, her granddaughter was smart. I didn't feel smart and didn't want to disappoint her. I was sure I was going to fail Standard 7 and would have to start over in Standard 5. Each day I went to class hoping to understand the lessons, hoping my wayward thoughts would come running back, but each day I left feeling despondent. I would forget about my troubles by the time I got home, only to be reminded of them the next day. *Was I going to be left behind?* I wondered.

13

A Christmas Gift

A few days before Christmas of 1977, I woke up to greet an ordinary day. The year had already been full of excitement, and it didn't intend to stop. With alarm clock precision, the rooster in our yard and all the others in the village had belted out their choruses in cadence with the rising sun. I joined them as I bounded out to the living room. But I was met by an unexpected sight that made me rethink my assumptions about the day. There was a grip (suitcase) in the living room. *What was my grandmother planning now?* I had to know.

When I asked her about it, she replied in her usual matter of fact way.

"Jacqueline, you're going to Canada."

There was no build up to the punch line. I wasn't too surprised; I knew I'd go to Canada to see my mother one day—that she'd "send for me." I yawned, wiped the sleep from my eyes, and took the bait.

"When am I going to Canada?"

"You're going to Canada today."

My grandmother's fishing hook, if you will, delivered a jolt that left me completely awake and dangling in confusion.

"Today…? I'm going to Canada, today?"

"Yes. You're going to see your mother for a few days."

There wasn't a lot of time to ask questions or get ready and that was exactly how my grandmother planned it. I was floured and frying in the pan before I could blink twice. I was soon garnished and ready for presentation, ready to go to see my mother.

My big day had come, at long last! It felt like Santa finally delivered a present for me, and oh, what a present it was. I'd met and spent time with my father, and now I was going to see my mother, whom I'd only seen in pictures. Plus, I'd get a break from some of the challenges that I'd encountered with my late transition to Standard 7, after returning from England.

But, as with my visit to England, I didn't say bye to my father, my friends, relatives or neighbours. That was also how my grandmother planned it; nobody was going to "work obeah" on her plans. It was only a visit, though, so I could tell them about it when I returned, including my cousin Olivene. She was surprised to learn that I was on my way to Canada.

My grandmother told me the pilot and stewardesses (now flight attendants) would take care of me. She and my aunt/sister weren't going with me this time, but I wasn't afraid. All those times that I went to Bethel, ran errands, the time I went home from Plymouth by myself, and even my recent trip to England had prepared me well. I was fine travelling alone at ten years old—the "unaccompanied minor" experience. It was like that of the children in the movie by the same name, minus the wild airport escapades. Well, my adventures happened later.

Come with me to Blackburne Airport, where I expected to climb the stairs of the LIAT airplane. Instead, you'll see me boarding a small plane as I waved goodbye to my family and headed to Canada. As it was the middle of December, it was an almost sure way to experience a baptism by snow and temperatures cold enough to chill my bones. But I wasn't concerned about snow. I was full of wonder as I climbed into the plane, relieving my family of the burden of paying the fare for an accompanying adult.

"Good morning. Welcome onboard!" the pilot said as I entered the plane.

"Good morning."

"Would you like to sit in the co-pilot's seat, next to me?"

"Yes!" I said, with as much enthusiasm as a shy ten-year-old could muster.

I settled in beside him. There were probably two additional seats on the plane, but I don't remember seeing other passengers. I'd never been in a small plane like that or sat at the front with the pilot so I was giddy with excitement, although he probably couldn't tell. I also couldn't wait to see Canada, and my mother. I'd communicated with her via mail but hadn't seen or spoken with her since I was two-and-a-half years old. I would have so many stories about "away" to tell the rest of my family and friends, when I returned home in a couple of weeks.

"Jacqueline, Canada is a cold place," my grandmother had told me. "You have to wear a few vests under your dress so that you won't feel cold."

"Yes, Mama."

"Sometimes people in Canada are buried in their houses in the snow and can't get out for days," she explained.

Canada probably looked like the postcards relatives sent us, with snowy houses and children playing outside in puffy clothes. They looked like they were having fun, so I wasn't concerned. Soon, I would see snow and also my mother. She had married and had two children, so I would meet her husband and my two younger sisters as well.

"Jacqueline, your mother's husband is a Jamaican," my grandmother also told me. "I don't like him at all! Don't you ever marry a Jamaican!"

Why didn't my grandmother like him? I wondered. She didn't like my father either, but I liked him. *Maybe I'll also like my mother's husband...*

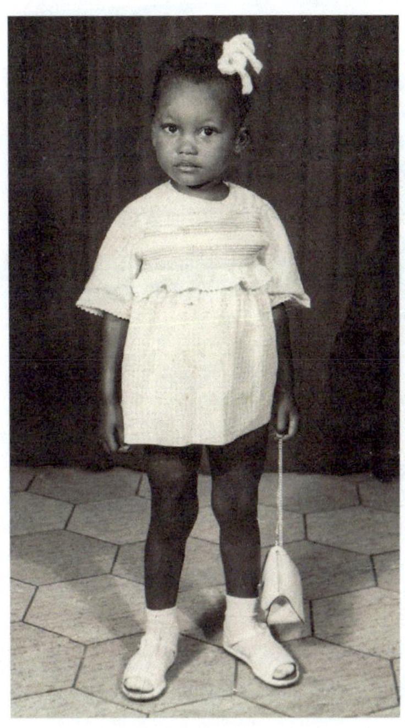

This is me, at two-and-a-half.

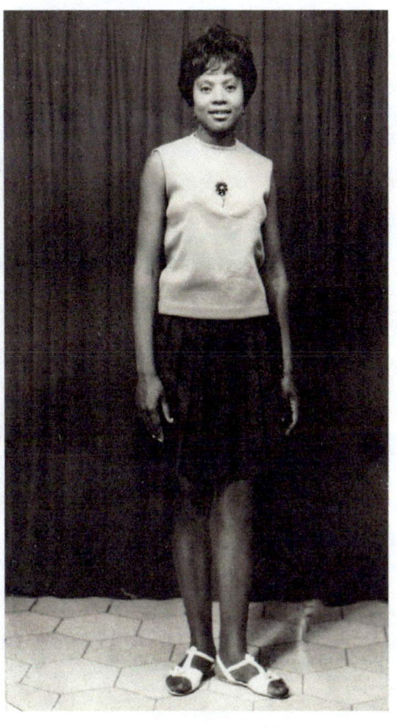

This is my mother, likely preparing to emigrate to Canada.

This is my maternal grandmother—Mama.

This is my maternal great grandmother—Granny.

Here, I am with my cousin (Tracy), aunt/sister (Brenda) and uncle (Cecil), facing our house, with the cloud-covered Soufrière Hills in the background. Our dog, Hero, looked on.

This is our house in Harris, with the concrete extension, including the veranda.

Here, my father is standing beside his tour bus,
which displays his nickname, "Nice."

Here is my paternal aunt (Irene) whom I met when I was an adult
and my paternal grandfather (Isaac) whom I've never met.

This is my maternal grandmother— Mama. She may have taken this picture while we were in England, in 1977.

Part 2

Canada

14

Oh Canada

I was finally in Canada, the place that had occupied my dreams for so long. We landed at the Toronto International Airport (now Lester B. Pearson International Airport, named after Canada's 14th prime minister).

"Would you recognize your mother, if you saw her?" a woman asked, once the stewardess transitioned me to her care.

"Yes, I would recognize her. I had pictures of her in Montserrat."

"Okay, let's go and meet your mother."

I was eager to see her. We went out to an area where there were a lot of people, and she stopped and asked me,

"Do you see your mother?"

There were so many people; I kept looking at them, looking for a woman with an afro. I looked and looked again but didn't see anyone who looked like my mother. As I began to wonder if she had come to the airport yet, the person accompanying me turned to me.

"She is right there," she said gently, pointing to where my mother was standing.

I still didn't see her. Then, out of the sea of people a voice said,

"Are you going to say hello and give your mother a hug?"

Oh...this is my mother?

She'd been "away" so long, I didn't recognize her; I couldn't see whether she had an afro, as she had on a thick hat. An immigration officer spoke with my mother, who signed something, and transitioned me to her care. I wasn't afraid. She seemed like a nice person, but I didn't know her. She wasn't like my father, though; she didn't keep hugging me and holding my hand, and that was fine with me. One touchy-feely parent was more than enough. But meeting my father, who was also like a stranger to me, meeting him at eight years old, had probably prepared me to meet my mother.

We went into the familiar rectangular box—this time I knew we weren't being weighed. As we headed from the airport, I don't recall if the ground was white with snow, and I wasn't bothered by the cold. I barely noticed a big difference in temperature. I was glad people didn't seem to be buried in their houses, though. I also don't remember what my mother and I talked about. As usual, I wasn't talkative, and my aunt/sister and grandmother weren't with me to help carry the conversation. My mother probably did most of the talking as I answered her questions.

Once we arrived at the apartment in North York, I got settled. My mother asked me to change into other clothes.

"Why are you wearing so many vests, she asked?" as I took off my clothes.

"Mama said Canada's cold, so I had to dress properly," I explained.

Smiling, she opened my grip.

"Where are your clothes?" she asked.

"I don't know."

My grandmother hadn't packed my clothes, only items for my mother. It's a good thing my mother had some clothes for me.

I finally met my two young sisters and my mother's husband, who came home a short time later. Her husband said hello and wasn't talkative, other than telling me a few house rules. I wasn't talkative with him either but made a mental note of the rules.

Don't touch the organ.

Don't touch the stereo.

Don't touch the vinyl records.

We didn't have any of those things at my house in Montserrat. But I didn't do what I did at Vue Pointe Hotel when I kept touching things that my uncle told me not to touch. I was older by then; I obeyed the rules and tried not to make him unhappy.

• • •

I did touch the snow when I went outside with my mother and sisters later. But it was as if I'd grown up with snow because it didn't seem strange to me. My grandmother had told me so many times about people buried in their house who couldn't get out for days; I was relieved to see that all the nearby houses and buildings were visible, and that snow was nice and fluffy and no one seemed to be too bothered by it—of course I didn't have to shovel or drive in it; I seemed to be able to adapt to a new environment relatively quickly. My mother must have also ensured that I was dressed warmly as I don't recall feeling too cold.

I was okay with snow, and there were a few other things that I liked. I was pleasantly surprised by warm showers (we didn't have warm water in Montserrat and England only had baths). I liked red apples. It was Christmas time so I liked seeing the lights on the Christmas tree, and I think I even had a couple of presents under the tree. But, on Christmas Day, when my stepfather asked my sisters what Santa brought for them, I remembered what my grandmother said: "Santa isn't real." Plus, my mother, who seemed as practical as my grandmother, told me that the present was from her. And I think another person had also sent a gift for me.

I enjoyed spending time with my Uncle Basil and his family; he was still as cool as he was when he visited us in Montserrat. I had a strong connection with him. I'd also met some of my mother's friends and other family members, and they were all very nice. I didn't know about the important conversations she was having with them, though.

To my surprise, my mother had decided that I'd stay in Canada, after consulting with family and friends. My mother sent a message to my grandmother to let her know I wasn't returning to Montserrat. She would have left the message with either the police station in Harris or our neighbour, Mrs. Ponde, one of the few places/people with telephones in our village. I don't remember feeling happy or sad about hearing that I was staying in Canada. I also didn't know how long it would be before I saw, or even spoke with, my grandmother or father or other family and friends again. I didn't feel sad about this either. Again, I seemed to be able to adapt easily. My mother told me that she was working out the details for my stay. I imagined her talking to a stern, nicely dressed white man, as my grandmother had when planning our visit to England.

Sponsoring me was likely easier than I imagined, though. Per the West Indian Domestic Scheme immigration policy, under which my mother immigrated to Canada, she could get landed immigrant status after working in Canada for one year, sponsor her relatives, and ultimately obtain citizenship.

Although sponsorship was relatively easy, finalizing the paperwork would take time. In the meantime, I couldn't attend school. I started worrying about how many classes I'd missed and whether I'd be able to catch up. It was my biggest concern, although I was still adjusting to my stepfather; he didn't seem happy about me staying, based on conversations that I overheard. The bone-chilling temperatures I anticipated in Canada seemed to come from within my new home, and not from outside. My stepfather didn't really speak to me, and, if he did, it wasn't pleasant.

I experienced another unpleasantry, after a visit to the doctor's, which made me a little concerned about worms. Okay—a lot concerned! The doctor's appointment was probably standard for immigrants. It included a physical examination of the usual things: height and weight measurements, eyes and skin checks, and a stool test. Once the results were ready, the doctor informed me and my mother that I had parasites—microscopic worms!

His words sent shockwaves through my body. I'd been very careful in Montserrat and was confused about how I got them. I thought that I'd followed the instructions a nurse had provided when she visited us at St. Georges Primary School, to educate us about the importance of hygiene.

"Children, make sure you wash your hands often, and before you eat."

"Yes, Nurse."

"Let me tell you the story about a girl who didn't practice proper hygiene."

"Yes, Nurse."

"A girl had worms and they came out of her body through her stool."

Wide eyes.

"They also tried to come out through her mouth and ended up getting stuck in her throat."

Wider eyes and opened mouths.

I don't remember if the nurse said they choked her to death or almost did, but after hearing that story, I was surely motivated to keep my hands clean. I'd seen someone poo in the bushes, as we did sometimes as children, and long, large, white worms came out in the poo. The story that the nurse told us made me connect that experience with hygiene. I tried to avoid getting worms. But now the doctor was telling me that I had them!

He explained that it was common for children from the Caribbean to have worms and that he'd give me medication to pass them. *Pass them?*

"Will I...see them?" I managed to ask.

"No, they're microscopic," he explained. "You won't see them."

I was relieved to hear that, but was still concerned. Each time I had the urge to poo, I froze; images of my friend with the worms came to mind. I held it in as long as possible but was no match for the powerful peristalsis waves and rectal muscles that forced me to the throne. I didn't linger there, though, as I needed to do a quick check.

Is anything moving? Please don't let me see anything moving...

Feeling relieved when I didn't see any worms, I quickly washed up, wiped the sweat from my brow and waited, with dread, for the next episode.

After a few weeks of treatment, futile battles with biological functions, and anxiety-filled imagining of all possible worst-case scenarios, I finally breathed a sigh of relief. The doctor was right. I didn't see any worms, and I was happy when he confirmed that my unwelcomed, invisible companions were gone (cue the Hallelujah song from Handel's *Messiah!)*

I was also relieved when all the immigration paperwork was finally sorted out. By then, I'd turned 11. I don't recall how I celebrated my birthday, but unlike how I'd previously celebrated with my grandmother, there was definitely no Perkins/Perks Rum Punch involved, although I did miss those moments with her. I was more focused on getting registered for school than celebrating, though.

What will school in Canada be like?

Will I like my teachers and schoolmates?

Will I be able to catch up?

15

Re-setting, With Gratitude

In winter 1978, a few months after coming to Canada, I walked with my mother from our apartment down to the nearby Brookbanks Public School (now Crestwood Preparatory College). She was taking me to get registered. The winter of 1977–78 was intense, with blizzards and very cold temperatures, but it didn't seem to bother me. I liked looking at all the snow as we walked to Brookbanks; my mother must have continued to dress me warmly as I don't remember feeling cold. We arrived relatively quickly and were soon walking down the hallway to the office, which seemed very long to me, back then.

My mother spoke with the principal, who was tall, white, and friendly looking; he didn't seem strict like our headmaster in Montserrat. I sat quietly in a chair, near the opened office door. A girl who looked like me (and about the same age as me) poked her head through the door.

"Hi! I'm Sharon. Do you want to be my friend?"

No one had ever asked me that before, likely because everyone knew everyone in my village, in Montserrat.

"Yes," I replied to Sharon.

I didn't think saying no was an option, though. Satisfied with my answer, she said a few more things to me, then skipped off.

Meanwhile, my mother finished talking to the principal, who had come over to say hello and welcome me. I'd learned from her that Canada used the term "grades" instead of "standards." My biggest concern was what grade I was going to be in...

My wondering was soon interrupted with a strange interaction.

"Jacqueline, do you have any questions?"

I don't think anyone had ever asked me if I had questions about anything, ever. Despite my amazement, I managed to open my mouth and ask one.

"What grade will I be in?"

"You'll be in Grade 5," he replied. "Why do you ask?"

"I'd skipped two standards in Montserrat and was in Standard 7."

"We don't do that here. Are you going to be okay to go to Grade 5?"

"Yes," I said, feeling relieved. No one had asked how I *felt* about anything before.

Looking back, I realize how privilege, or the lack thereof, impacted our lives. In our village, my family didn't enjoy most of the privileges that some families in Canada, other countries, or even the middle- and upper-class families in Montserrat enjoyed. We didn't have many material things, and my grandmother, aunts, and uncles had to do a lot of physical labour. They had to work on the land, and, before we got plumbing, they had to carry water home from the Bugby Hole River on their heads (a technique that our enslaved ancestors also used). My family didn't have the time or energy to ask me how I felt about anything—it wasn't a priority. Plus, the colonial notion about children being seen and not heard meant I wasn't likely to be asked my opinion.

It was nice to be asked how I felt and whether I had questions, but my interaction with the principal still made me wonder about a few things.

Did my grandmother tell my mother that I was failing miserably in Standard 7?

Is that why she decided to keep me in Canada?

Is that why they decided to put me in Grade 5?

I learned later that my mother hadn't known that I wasn't doing well in Standard 7, and it was unlikely my teacher approached my grandmother to discuss the matter. Maybe the headmaster thought I was doing fine and wasn't as worried as I was. After all, I kept getting lashes from my Standard 4 teacher for not understanding things and still managed to get a high mark—and go on to *skip two standards.* I didn't have to worry about my Standard 7 woes anymore; I was happy and a little nervous about starting Grade 5.

• • •

My mother walked with me to school every day for a few weeks. She also picked me up for lunch and took me back to school after lunch. One day, I quickly walked home for lunch before she could leave to get me. She was surprised to see me at the door of our apartment.

"After walking to and from school with you a few times, I know the way now," I attempted to explain.

After getting this glimpse of my independent, problem-solving personality, she stopped dropping me off and picking me up entirely. My grandmother had trained me well, at least. Walking near buildings, houses, other students, and a crossguard, was much easier than walking to Bethel Village—near cows, bulls, bushes, and possibly Fine Twine, the criminal on the run.

Sharon also walked to school, so sometimes I met up with her, and we walked together. On the first day of school, she introduced me to her friends. She made space for me—invited me into the group. I didn't have concerns about being included or adjusting to new friends; looking back, I realize that things could have gone differently, had I not been accepted. Sharon's inclusive mindset helped me adjust quickly.

Our group included a couple of Black girls (me and Sharon), an Italian girl, a Greek girl, and a white girl I think was Canadian-born. However, it could have been possible that they were all born in Canada and simply the children of immigrants. There were others who were immigrants, or children of immigrants, including East Asian, South Asian, and Caribbean students. Everyone seemed to get along. My teacher was nice and made me feel welcomed. She was white—in fact, I think all the teachers at Brookbanks were white, but I didn't notice it then. I was more focused on adjusting to my new environment. I'd become astute at assessing people's characters, and the first thing I could tell was whether they were kind or compassionate. My teacher passed my subconscious character test; her whiteness wasn't relevant to me.

Of course, I'm now more aware of unconscious bias and systemic barriers that have made race relevant. We're slowly making progress on structural changes in education and other sectors—changes that will help us become better local and global citizens, and mitigate the repetition of racist practises and systems. Some schools have updated curricula to include the history of Canada's Black and Indigenous people.

Our Parliament made some symbolic changes as well. Black History Month honours contributions of Black Canadians and recognizes injustices over which we've triumphed, and the contributions we continue to make—the Honourable Jean Augustine, who came to Canada from Grenada, under the West Indian Domestic Scheme, Rosemary Sadlier, and the Honourable Donald H. Oliver, helped to establish this law. September 30 is the National Day of Truth and Reconciliation so that we never forget the injustices perpetrated against Canada's first peoples. It is a day to honour First Nations, Inuit, and Métis children who were taken from their homes and communities to attend residential schools run by the federal government—some didn't survive. There was a small change to the Canadian national anthem to make the lyrics more inclusive, and there are other changes underway; civil rights pioneer Viola Desmond has been featured on our $10 bill.

At the start of class, we sang the old version of the anthem and said the Lord's Prayer; I knew the latter, of course, as we did the same in Montserrat. As we settled into class to start our lessons, I was relieved that my new teacher didn't have a strap for administering punishment. There was no assembly or in-class dramatic show. Although I missed my friends and family, I didn't miss getting lashes at all. At Brookbanks, punishment for students who misbehaved was time in the principal's office. This made sense to me as I remembered how effective my father's style of discipline was: scolding and time out. Even though Brookbanks and other schools didn't use corporal punishment, it wouldn't be completely abolished in Canada until many years later.

Without the fear of punishment, I was able to focus on learning. During a lesson, our teacher showed us how to do long division.

"Do you understand, Jacqueline?" she came to my desk to ask.

"No, I don't. I understand short but not long division."

She seemed surprised, but took the time to show me how to do it. She didn't send me to the board to test if I understood the lesson, and then punish me if I didn't. After seeing her work through a couple of problems, I understood and started feeling more confident. I also learned to capture point-form notes and use "paraphrasing" for a research project. It was my first time doing that work; she again took the time to explain and after a few tries I got the hang of it.

I also enjoyed participating in the Health Hustle, which involved exercising to music. My teacher led the sessions as we hustled to songs that I'd never heard: "Bad Bad Leroy Brown" and "Tie a Yellow Ribbon Round the Ole Oak Tree." It was a lot of fun.

I'll forever be grateful for my teacher's patience, kindness, and warm spirit. She helped me adjust to school in Canada, including Picture Day, which I experienced for the first time—my Grade 5 individual and class pictures are still my favourite school pictures. Most importantly, she helped me fill my educational gaps, resulting from an unfortunate situation.

16

Option Three: Run!

We lived in a diverse community of immigrants in a mixed-income neighbourhood. Some people lived in government subsidized housing, some in market rent apartments, and others lived in houses. It was a safe area and a nice community, but even in a nice area you'll find both good people and unwelcome creatures.

After finishing Grade 5, I enjoyed my first summer and first party in Canada. Sharon lived in an apartment nearby, and I accepted the invitation to her birthday party. One of my cousins in Montserrat, who lived in a very large house, in another village, had parties on her birthday. I'd been to one or two of them but didn't take a gift. I remember that she had a cake, and there were decorations and we played outside and in her room. The extent of my own birthday celebrations was a capful of Rum Punch, so I had a limited frame of reference for birthday parties.

Sharon was bold and asked us what presents we were going to bring for her. Based on her question, I realized that I had to bring something. I didn't have a gift, so I made one. My mother had purchased hair accessories and some had multiple items so I took some from different packages and put them in a little box. I covered it with the cartoon section of the newspaper and was very pleased with my ingenuity.

Sharon's apartment was nicely decorated, and there were a lot of people as well as a lot to eat and drink. Everyone was dressed in fancy clothes and I wasn't—I felt a little out-of-place. I made a mental note: *wear nicer clothes for the next party!* Sharon's friends brought a lot of gifts, which were all nicely wrapped. I felt embarrassed about my gift so I held on to it and made another mental note: *better wrapping paper, next time!*

When it was time to open gifts, I was surprised to see that children had brought her jewellery and other nice things. To stall as long as possible, I told Sharon,

"I'll give you the gift that I brought for you a little later."

"Okay."

In truth, I hoped that she'd forget that I had a gift. She didn't. After she opened all her gifts, she invited me to go to her room so that I could give her the gift, in private. When I finally gave it to her, she wondered why I didn't want to do so in front of everyone. She was very appreciative and genuinely seemed to like it. Nothing ever seemed to bother her, though. I admired that about Sharon and was grateful for her attitude. I looked forward to seeing her more, and my other friends, as we headed into the new school year.

• • •

In Grade 6, our teacher wasn't as approachable as our Grade 5 teacher, but he was also not like my headmaster in Montserrat, so

I couldn't complain. I continued to learn and build skills. During breaks (recess) at school, people skated on the ice rink in the schoolyard. I was fascinated as I watched their effortless gliding.

I wanted to learn to skate and asked my mother for skates, which she purchased for me. One day, I strapped them on, and Sharon and my other friends taught me how to skate. My first lesson was to learn to stand on the ice. It was much more slippery than I expected but I was determined to learn. My friends held my hands as I pushed forward. I thought I'd gotten the hang of it... so they let go. I kept gliding, not knowing how to stop—then fell. I provided a lot of entertainment each time I fell. But I improved and was soon zipping around at the school rink and on trips to nearby rinks.

I took on a leadership role during sports, like volleyball, by calling out plays and encouraging my team. Surprising to me, but not to anyone else, competition helped me continue to find my voice and become more assertive. I learned to play some musical instruments, and I played the best scary tree in the Wizard of Oz. I was disappointed that I didn't get the part of Dorothy, but I made the most of the role I was given and showed off my acting skills for my mother and sisters who came to see the play.

My mother approved for me to go on a Grade 6 trip to Madawaska Valley, Ontario—my first overnight school trip. We stayed there for two or three days and participated in outdoor lessons, learning about trees, plants, and rocks. I enjoyed the feeling of independence, of being away from home, and the fun activities such as roasting marshmallows and singing around campfires. I learned camp songs like "Quarter Master's Store," about mice running through rice and rats as big as alley cats, at the Quarter Master's Store.

Mice and rats were popular in school and campfire songs in Canada, as they were in songs and nursery rhymes in Montserrat; we used to sing "Three Blind Mice." However, during my short time in Canada, I also learned that rats of the human kind were not unique to Montserrat.

• • •

One day, during the summer after I completed Grade 6, I was in the playground outside my apartment building. It was enclosed with a chain link fence and a gate. I was the only one in the playground; as an introvert, I didn't mind playing by myself. I was on the swing near the side that was farthest away from the gate, when a man approached me. He was in casual clothing, well-groomed, and seemed nice. He walked up to the fence on the outside of the playground, leaned on it, and started speaking to me.

"Hello," he said in a gentle voice, as if trying to reassure me that he was trustworthy.

It didn't work, as my previous experiences told me otherwise. My internal alarm bell (my rat-dar, if you will) was sounding off loudly. I kept swinging, and per my usual strategy, I remained calm and started thinking about possible solutions.

Option one: Keep swinging and hope that he leaves.

Option two: Tell him to leave me alone.

Option three: Run.

He likely misinterpreted my silence as a willingness to engage with him. In his "nice" voice, he asked me to come and talk to him, as if I just needed a little encouragement to take the next step. I still didn't respond and was now calculating distance and speed for implementing option three. We were both about the same distance away from the gate but on opposite sides.

How quickly could I get to the gate and then to the building door, and would he try to follow me? I wondered. I would have to run to the door quickly, open it, then run inside. For a brief moment, I might be hidden from sight, as the door was under a balcony. I had to take the chance—and if he tried to follow me, I would scream loudly.

He was probably also mindful of the balconies and wouldn't risk someone seeing him grab me or looking suspicious, which is likely why he kept his distance and tried to look casual. He was counting on my naivety and had no idea how prepared I was to handle him.

After a quick evaluation of the options, I chose option three. I slowed down the swing, slowly got off, and waited a couple of seconds to see what he'd do. He stayed in the same position and didn't say anything. I casually and slowly started walking towards the gate of the playground while observing him peripherally. He turned his head in my direction and followed me with his eyes but didn't move.

This was a good sign, I thought. Maybe he thought that I was going out to speak to him. I tried not to make any sudden movements, to reduce the chances of him reacting. Opening the gate slowly, I paused, and then bolted to the door while doing periodic checks to see what he was doing. Quickly opening the door, I rushed in and ensured that it closed behind me. I made it! My heart was beating out of my chest as I kept running down the hallway. I ran past the first-floor laundry room and elevator, past the lobby and first floor apartment units, and up the stairs to my apartment unit. Yeah, I was pretty certain that he was a rat of the human kind.

Feeling shaken, I went to my room. My stepfather was home, but I didn't speak with him about it; Our relationship hadn't progressed since my first day in Canada. He still didn't speak to me very much. I was sure that he didn't like me, and the feeling was mutual. I'd concluded and accepted that our relationship was going to be similar to the relationship that I had with my aunt's/sister's father, back in Montserrat.

My mother was home, but I didn't want to speak with her, either. I was repeating the pattern of not speaking to an adult about the bad people that I encountered. If I told her about the man, I would have to explain why I thought he was a rat, but I didn't want to discuss my experiences in Montserrat with her, yet. It would be years before I told her about them, but I was soon forced to tell her about this one.

Later that day, a police officer came to our door. I don't know if he was knocking on all the doors or if he came specifically to our apartment unit. My mother called me.

"Jackie [she shortened my name], this officer is looking for a man. He's checking to see if anyone has seen him."

The officer described him, and he fit the description of the man that I saw.

"A man was trying to talk to me while I was in the playground, but I left and didn't talk to him," I told the officer.

My mother heard it for the first time and was surprised. The officer said that it was probably the same man and that he was a suspect, so if I saw him again, I should stay away, get help, and call the police. I never saw him again, and I don't know if the police ever found him. I was grateful that he wasn't successful in harming me, and I hope that he didn't harm anyone else.

17

Breaking Point

I started Grade 7 at Donview Heights Junior High School (now Donview Middle School). But it wasn't like when I skipped from Standard 4 to Standard 7 in Montserrat, just before immigrating to Canada. Brookbanks Elementary School didn't have a skipping process, so starting school in Grade 5 had allowed me to reset—adjust to the new school system and better prepare for Grade 7.

In my home classroom, we sang the National Anthem, said the Lord's Prayer, then listened to our teacher make an announcement about a swap.

"Okay, everyone. Some of you will go to another class, and students from another home room will come to our class."

The person who sat beside me was swapped and headed out. Soon, students from the other class shuffled in. I noticed a girl with a bubbly personality walking towards me. I could tell that her personality was very different from mine. She seemed to have so much energy; I didn't think we'd get along.

"Hi! I'm Mitsy," she said, settling into the seat beside me.

As with my experience with Sharon, it wasn't long before Mitsy and I became great friends. We adjusted well to junior high school (Grades 7 to 9), and our group of friends continued to expand (Michelle, Julie, Lav and others).

• • •

Our typing teacher was quirky, so we had fun in her class, learning to type on mechanical typewriters, and not in the watching-your-fingers way. They were loud and clunky, but I liked hearing the rhythmic clicking and clanking as we practised. It drowned out some of the comments, especially from boys who didn't feel comfortable learning to type because it was "women's work." I focused on the lessons and made progress each time the keys/hammers hit the paper and the bell "dinged" at the end of a line. With each keystroke and push of the lever to begin a new line, I increased my speed. By the end of the year, our teacher had survived any jokes and horsing around, and her sweet revenge was that I and other students were typing very fast—she'd whipped us into shape in spite of ourselves.

It would be a few years before the launch of the internet, and, eventually, the World Wide Web—something we hadn't imagined then and can't imagine living without now. We'd eventually appreciate those typing skills and use them to interact efficiently with computers and even mobile phones. But, in the meantime, we put our new skills and tools to good use.

"Hey, I typed the lyrics to a couple of songs!" one of our friends said.

"Whoa...you typed 'Rapper's Delight' by The Sugarhill Gang and 'Another One Bites the Dust' by Queen?"

"Yeah!"

We were very intrigued with the rap and funk-rock genres. We'd huddle during recess with papers in hand, memorizing the two 1979 hits. We sang/rapped with enthusiasm and passion, as one of our friends played the music on his ginormous ghetto blaster (boom box). We had so much fun.

Eventually, we transitioned to listening to music on smaller devices like the Walkman, Discman, and iPod. But ghetto blasters were our thing back then, and some are still around today.

My mother had a rule about secular music, though: we weren't supposed to listen to it. It may have come from the church that we attended—West End Revival (now Prayer Palace), similar to the Pentecostal church I used to visit in Montserrat. My mother had joined my stepfather's church instead of a Methodist church. The congregation was diverse, and the pastor was white and charismatic. He sang and moved like Elvis Presley, stopping short of the hip thrusts.

I'd come to like Elvis almost as much as my cousin in England did. I also liked other secular music—in Montserrat, my non-digital playlist included religious, secular, and cultural music. But some religions consider cultural music to be secular, which sometimes has the effect of suppressing culture. My stepfather listened to secular music too—one of the few things that we had in common. I knew this because my sisters used to tattle on him. Sometimes, they busted through the apartment door, like investigative reporters who'd uncovered the most incredible story. I would hear the excitement in their little voices as they reported their findings:

"Mommy! Daddy was listening to disco music in the car!"

He would playfully ask them why they talked so much.

I didn't have a good relationship with him and didn't think to use our common like of different genres of music to connect. Instead, I avoided him by staying late at school for basketball practises and games. Sometimes, I hung out at Mitsy's house eating bully (corned) beef and rice. We'd talk/support each other and watch the Young and the Restless—good thing our friendship worked out.

As for my stepfather, I barely spoke to him. Surprisingly, he wasn't a stickler for honorifics, so when I did speak to him, I used his first name, per his request. He was strict about cleaning the apartment early on Saturday mornings, though—that was the rule when he was growing up in Jamaica. When my mother was home on Saturdays, before we cleaned, she and I, and sometimes my sisters, had a ritual of sitting or kneeling on our plastic-covered couch for devotion—covering couches was common for many people who immigrated from the Caribbean and other countries. They worked hard for their material possessions and made sure they lasted as long as possible, even if it meant they, or guests, weren't always comfortable sitting on them.

We spent many Saturday mornings on that couch reading the Bible and praying—it was both our seat and altar. After devotion, we peeled ourselves off the plastic and ate a tasty breakfast. It was usually liver, kidney, salt fish or corned beef with Johnny cakes (Montserratian fried dumplings), which my mother prepared so well. After breakfast, it was time to clean, while my sisters watched cartoons. My chores were to clean the plastic on the couches, vacuum, dust, polish the furniture, sweep the floor, and more.

• • •

On a Saturday (cleaning) morning, when I was about 13 years old, I was in my room nursing a nosebleed; I started getting them after immigrating to Canada. My mother was at work, and my stepfather was talking to his friend in the living room. I heard his footsteps pounding on the parquet floor as he marched down the hallway and stopped abruptly at the door to my room. He wasn't happy that I hadn't started cleaning and demanded that I get going.

"My nose is bleeding, I need a few minutes," I explained. It had barely stopped, so I was waiting to make sure it didn't restart, before going about my day. He insisted that I clean right away. I reacted and copped a teenage attitude:

"I'll clean later!"

Understandably, he didn't like my attitude, and his response was good old-fashioned Caribbean discipline. I probably deserved some discipline, but I thought it was excessive—hard lashes, pushes, hits. I knew a thing or two about lashes but had never experienced anything like it, in terms of intensity and physical and emotional impact. In addition, it had been about three years since anyone lashed me in school or at home, so it was a shock to my senses.

Some might argue for not sparing the rod and spoiling the child; some Caribbean folk might even kiss their teeth (chups) at my argument that hard lashes are extreme. We chupsed when we disagreed with something, were vexed (upset or annoyed), or thought something was utter foolishness. We also chupsed playfully in response to silly jokes or situations. It was usually done in front of the person or people to whom it was directed, but we would be careful when chupsing around adults as that could end with a box (slap).

Regardless, I picked myself up off the floor, where I'd ended up—it had all happened so fast—and called my mother at work, hyperventilating. I could barely speak, as I explained what happened. Later, I sat quietly at our neighbour's house, listening as my mother and the neighbour discussed the situation and tried to find a solution—she'd told me to go there until she got home. They didn't seem to find one but likely continued to discuss things. I got the impression that there was nothing they could do, though. That terrified me as I sensed that there was more of that "discipline" in my future…that things were going to get worse.

My independent, problem-solving nature kicked in once again, and I started brainstorming. I remembered an incident when I verbally stood up for myself at school, and where, consequently, some students had generously, but inappropriately, bestowed me with honorary physical fighting skills. The incident had happened in Grade 5 when we were lining up to go into our classroom. I was first in line and was standing there minding my business, when a boy cut in front of me.

"I'm going to be first in line!" he said.

"No, you're not. I'm first in line," I calmly responded.

"I'm going to keep standing here, so what are you going to do about it?" he insisted.

"Keep standing there, and you'll see what I do about it."

I was bluffing, surprised by the words coming out of my mouth. My heart started racing and I hoped that he'd just move away. I'd never been in a physical fight but found myself preparing to use a physical fight strategy. Looking back, I remember when I thought someone in my village had hurt my grandmother, how I wanted to find and hurt that person in return. Maybe I was more of a fighter than I thought. At some point in our lives, we figure out the best way to handle challenges, which come in different forms and different people, though they all have the same thing in common—your needs versus mine, and how we're going to negotiate and compromise to meet them.

At some point we also get tired of running—from dogs, boys with snakes, paedophiles. Maybe I'd finally learned to be as bold as my aunt/sister. Maybe I perceived myself to be equal in strength or stronger than the boy who'd confronted me because I was, at least, taller than him. In fact, there were only two or three students who were taller than me. I was tall enough for a boy to call me "Jackie the ten-foot Packie." I didn't even know it was racist because in Montserrat, we made rhymes out of our friends' names, using the letter "P." My friends playfully called me Jacqueline Pacqueline, and my aunt/sister was Brenda Penda. So, "Jackie Packie" was perfectly normal to me, and I assumed the ten-foot reference was a silly, exaggerated way of indicating that I was unusually tall. It wasn't until years later that I learned that "Packie" was a racist word for South Asians.

But back to the boy who tried to cut in front of me, in line. As I stood there refusing to capitulate, and he stood there confused, he did the unexpected. To my relief, he started backing away, as he loudly proclaimed:

"Oooooh, don't mess with her! She can fight!"

"What?" *That's how it was going to end? It was that easy?*

He kept repeating it, that I could fight. It made me a little nervous because it couldn't have been further from the truth, but I didn't correct him. I figured the reputation could be advantageous, if someone challenged me in the future, which, of course, someone did.

It was probably the next day when a boy from my class walked up to me.

"I heard you can fight, so meet me after school and prove it."

This is how things went viral back then. It's amazing to me how a story, like the fact that I can fight, gained traction...how people filled in the blanks when they didn't have all the information.

"Okay!" I said confidently, not confident at all.

Later, a small crowd gathered in the schoolyard. A few of my friends were there, calmly chatting, waiting; I'd told them that I was challenged to a fight and needed their support. I knew better than to show up alone. Much sooner than I would have preferred, my opponent walked purposefully in my direction. My eyes slowly and nervously followed him, stopping abruptly as he stood face to face with me.

This boy could sit on me and squash me like a bug, I thought. He certainly had the mass and ability to do it; he was stout, and I was skinny. But I'd shown up for the fight. My strategy was to stand as tall as possible; that was easy to do. I was a tall 11-year-old; at least I was taller than him, even though we were the same age. Then I clung tightly to a hope and a prayer—that sweat beads wouldn't betray my shyness and fears, and that it would be over quickly.

As we locked eyes in a stare down, his warm breath greeted my face, as if warning of a bull about to charge. I maintained my stance and refused to back down. But what happened next surprised me and left me in a cloud of confusion.

What the heck just happened...? Am I dreaming...? To my surprise, he had backed away.

"Okay. I believe you. You can fight," he declared.

That was it? It was that easy?

I was two for two, without doing anything! Maybe he didn't want the reputation of "beating up a girl." My height and the fact that I had friends may have also worked to my advantage. Whatever his reason for walking away, I couldn't have been more relieved.

Things were different back then, though. We didn't get suspended or expelled for fights. We also didn't carry guns and knives to school; if a fight broke out, people fought with their fists, limbs, etc. We gathered to watch fights, but they were mano a mano, and no one was seriously injured. And, of course, "cyber" and "bullying" hadn't yet met to form a toxic, harmful pairing. Today, I'd rethink my strategy for handling bullies, though, like deciding when it's better to walk away (with confidence) and get help.

Ultimately, I used my new reputation and height advantage to stop some fights; thankfully, I never had to put my honorary fighting skills into action at school. After my experience with my stepfather, however, I decided to put them to good use at home.

I planned to physically defend myself—my short-term plan. I knew that I wouldn't be able to pack a big punch, but Tyler Perry's *Madea* might have approved of my effort. At least I wouldn't feel as helpless as I did when he caught me off guard. But I needed to do more.

From talking to some of my friends, I knew that step-parent and step-children relationships were challenging. Some families worked through them, even if they didn't always get things right. But most didn't cope well and ultimately imploded or exploded. From my perspective, our situation was the latter, so unbeknownst to my mother, I started working on a long-term plan. A path for myself. It made me feel a little hopeful.

18

In My Neighbourhood

Despite my issues at home, I continued to do well at school. I had great friends, and I liked my neighbourhood—it was safe and had nearby parks, grocery stores, a mall, good schools, and more. I'll take you on an imaginary tour. We'll walk east from my apartment on York Mills Road up to Victoria Park, turn right and go down to Ellesmere, cross the street, heading east, and head into Parkway Mall on the right.

I liked hanging out at the mall with my friends. We didn't have a lot of money, so we often walked the halls, window shopping, laughing, and carrying on. There were a couple of times when security had enough of our raucous behaviour and kicked us out. But when we were at the mall with our parents, we were on our best behaviour. My mother liked to shop at K-Mart and

Bi-Way, which were discount retail stores in the mall. I didn't like those stores, though; they didn't have Levi's, Jordache or other brands some of my friends wore. Like most children, I didn't appreciate my mother's thrifty strategy and that she was doing her best with her budget.

My friends and I also shopped at Parkwoods Village Plaza, which was closer to home. If we walked back from Parkway Mall and headed down Ellesmere, which turns into Parkwoods Village Drive, we'd eventually get to Brookbanks Drive. If we turned left and kept going down Brookbanks Drive, we'd eventually get to Brookbanks Elementary School. We'll turn right instead and go to Parkwoods Village Plaza.

There were a couple of variety stores there, where we loved to shop for junk food (definitely not salt and vinegar chips). There was a Dominion store, where my mother shopped for groceries, and a Shoppers Drug Mart, where she shopped for pharmacy and beauty products. I went shopping with her most of the time, but sometimes she sent me to buy things on my own. She'd give me instructions.

"Jackie, use coupons for these items on the list."

"Okay, mom."

"Toothpaste is on sale but if they don't have any in stock, ask for a rain check."

"Yes, mom."

What the heck is a rain check? I'd ask myself.

She'd explained that it would allow her to get the item at the sale price, when it's back in stock, even if it wasn't on sale then. I still couldn't grasp the concept at the time. My mental block was probably because it was reminiscent of when my grandmother sent me to buy bread at Miss Beebee's Bakery, without any money. But my mother gave me money; I just didn't like having to negotiate. I didn't realize that these experiences were teaching me important life skills. So, sometimes, after arriving home from a grocery run, I had to go right back out to get that rain check that I'd "forgotten."

• • •

In our four-storey apartment building, most people knew, or were familiar with, each other. I had friends in the building and babysat for one or two neighbours. If I forgot my keys, which I did a few times, I could ask the superintendent to let me in. Neighbours helped each other, like the time when I got my period for the first time. I sheepishly told my mother.

"Mom, my period started."

"Oh...okay. I don't have any pads; I'll ask our neighbour for some."

The neighbour lived right across the hallway, so I could hear the muffled sounds as my mother spoke with her. My face was flushed from embarrassment that the neighbour now knew about my period. Then, my mother came bounding in as if she was bringing treasures; the neighbour had given her the kind of pads you had to pin to your panty. I was glad to get something, but what was up with the pins!? At least my mother purchased the ones with the adhesive, later.

My stepfather's sister also lived in the building, so she was another neighbour with whom I interacted. I enjoyed playing tennis with her at a court nearby, and my mother sent me to sleep over at her apartment a few times. This was reminiscent of my grandmother sending me to sleep at neighbours' houses, though I didn't encounter any bad hosts in Canada. Many years later, when I was an adult, I asked my mother about her experience with neighbours in Montserrat.

"Mom, did you have to sleep at other people's houses when you were a child?"

"Yes."

I thought maybe she'd experienced some of the things that I had, so I finally told her about them; she was shocked. She didn't have the same experiences. My grandmother likely trusted her neighbours because her children hadn't been abused by them. After all, people left their doors unlocked, and some didn't even have locks. Things had changed when I was a child, or maybe I was an easy target because of my shy, quiet disposition.

I was still shy at 13 years old but was learning to be more assertive, probably out of necessity. My attitude had also started to change because that's how things work when you become a teenager: *I know more than you* or *all these rules are stifling.* My eyes and other body parts took on a persona of their own, sometimes without me even realizing. But my mother would enlighten me.

"You better fix that face and your attitude, or I'll fix it for you."

"Huh?"

I couldn't figure out what she was seeing. But my teenage attitude was eclipsed by my fighting attitude that emerged when I stood up to my stepfather.

19

Make the Call

My relationships at home continued to deteriorate. If I felt that my stepfather was unfairly accusing me of things or barking orders at me, I barked right back, and the chaos would begin. True to my plan (smart or not), I physically fought back when he tried to hit me. But I was no fool; I knew that I was outmatched, so I would run into the bathroom after landing at least one hit. Then, we'd yell insults back and forth as he pounded on the door.

"Little girl, you think you're a woman in this house?"

"No! Do you think you're a man?"

That would get him all riled up, but he would eventually calm down and leave, and I'd cautiously come back out. Things would be calmer...until the next episode.

I didn't spare my mother, either. I would talk back to her, too; what I really wanted was for her to do something about the situation. I didn't stop to try to at least consider her perspective. One time when I was rude to my mother, my stepfather came towards me to discipline me. I was close to the dining table, and when I looked down, I saw a pepper bottle so I quickly picked it up and said, "If you touch me, I will blind you with this pepper." Yup, I literally used "blind" as a verb. I could feel the steam coming from my ears, if you will, and he must have seen it, too. He backed off, continuing to complain about my attitude. My mother asked me to leave the house.

"Jackie, you better go outside for a few minutes to cool off."

"Fine."

Things got increasingly more violent and I got increasingly angrier. I remember showing up to school with a bump on my forehead. I was probably in Grade 8 or 9 (14 or 15 years old). A teacher called me to the office so that I could talk to a counsellor.

"Jacqueline, what happened to your head?"

"Oh…uh, I fell and…uh, I hit my head against a wall."

"Are you sure that's what happened?"

"Yes…I'm sure."

I could tell that she didn't believe me.

"Jacqueline, if you ever need to talk, come and see me anytime."

"Okay."

I didn't tell the counsellor the truth about my experiences at home because, in my mind, I was no stupid child. I'd heard about foster care and knew students who were in the system. Some of them told me about the terrible abuse that they experienced, so I knew that I didn't want to end up there; it seemed worse than my situation, and, besides, I had my own plans. So even though the counsellor reached out to me again, I never confided in her about my home situation. I did confide in a few of my friends, though, and continued to write out my plan: move out when I turn 16 years old (which I'd learned was when you could legally live on your own), get a job, figure out where to live and with whom. I didn't even realize the power of the plan—that writing it down meant that I could keep it top of mind, continuously update it, and thereby increase the probability of achieving it.

As Grade 9 wound down, and we eventually celebrated our graduation, I looked forward to heading into Grade 10 and turning 16 in a few months; the goal was to get to 16 in one piece.

From my mother's perspective, I was going through a rebellious phase. She tried a number of tactics to reign me in—groundings, physical punishments, lectures, and more, but nothing worked. Finally, as some Caribbean parents do when they're at their wits' end with their ungrateful, rebellious children, she brought out the big guns.

"I'm going to send you back to Montserrat!" she declared, in exasperation.

Well, that got my attention. Although "away" wasn't everything I'd hoped, there were some aspects that were good. And I was confident that I could define/shape my own experience, even if I didn't know exactly how at the time. If I had to go back to Montserrat, I didn't want it to be under shameful circumstances; I didn't want to be a pappy-show (spectacle). I wasn't sure if my mother was bluffing, though. So I decided to be better behaved, while continuing to plan my move.

Soon, I headed into Grade 10 at Victoria Park High School and within a few months, I turned 16. I made it in one piece! It was time to execute the plan. But, first, I made an important and pivotal call.

One day when no one was home, I picked up the phone and dialled (literally) the number for immigration. I don't remember how I thought to do so; I sometimes wonder if it was the counsellor at my junior high school who had given me the contact information. I vaguely remember her giving me a contact sheet with different help numbers, and I think one of them was probably a number for immigration.

"Hello," I said, once a nice-sounding immigration officer answered the phone.

She didn't fit my stereotype of the stern, white man my grandmother spoke with when planning our visit to England. She also didn't seem like the one that I imagined my mother speaking with when she sponsored me.

"I'm calling for a friend," I continued. I told her the story about my "friend," though she knew I was calling about my own situation.

"Jacqueline, I'm going to ask you to go to a place called Mercury Youth Services and first speak to a counsellor there. Can you do that?"

"Oh…yes, I can do that."

"Once you speak with them, they'll connect you back to me, or someone else who works with me, and we'll discuss next steps."

"Okay, thank you."

In the meantime, as if things weren't bad enough, I learned from my mother that my grandmother was dying. Unlike when my neighbour told me false information when I was a child in Montserrat, this time the news was accurate. The good thing is that it probably helped to distract my mother from the "send me back to Montserrat" warnings.

20

Everything's Going to Be Alright

In 1981, my grandmother fell ill in Montserrat. She was diagnosed with cancer. As Montserrat had some healthcare system limitations, she had to travel to England for treatment. She continued her stay there and recovered, but fell ill again while still in England, and by 1983, her prognosis was poor. At the time, I was still in Grade 10 at Victoria Park High School and was 16 years old—the age at which I planned to move out of my mother's and stepfather's apartment. But I'd have to put that plan on hold for a bit. It was exam time, but there was no question in my mind that I had to see my grandmother. I made arrangements with my teachers to complete assignments and exams and travelled from Canada to England with my mother.

I hadn't seen or spoken with my grandmother since leaving Montserrat; telecommunications weren't simple back then. I missed her and missed celebrations like Christmas Festival and food like goat water. At least I'd had the opportunity to go to Caribana in Canada a couple of times with my mother, before she decided to stop going. I was also so busy trying to navigate my home situation that visiting her in Montserrat hadn't been on my radar. My grandmother's impending death made me and my family get our priorities straight, though.

On arriving in England, we quickly got settled at my aunt's house before going to visit my grandmother at the hospital. I felt my heart racing as I saw her for the first time in years. I gave her a hug gently, seeing that she wasn't her usual strong self.

"You've grown so nicely Jacqueline…but you're still so skinny."

Per my grandmother's usual generalization, skinny people weren't happy, so this was code for you're still so unhappy. I wouldn't have expected to hear anything different, although she probably weighed less than I did at that point. Despite her failing health, she had a peaceful disposition, seemed even content. Psychologists and spiritual people might describe it as joy, a joy not dependent on how things are going.

"How are you doing in school? How are things?

"Everything's fine, Mama."

I wondered if she could tell that I wasn't being completely truthful; that "away" wasn't quite what I expected. I didn't want to burden her by telling her about my home situation, especially about my stepfather. She had told me that she didn't like him before I came to Canada. I'm sure hearing about the things that had transpired would have made her very upset.

"Where is the comb? Come and comb my hair for me, Jacqueline."

"Okay, Mama."

Her hair looked fine to me; she was likely trying to distract me from feeling sad. It was just like my grandmother to put me to work.

It was the first time that I'd ever combed her hair. She was the one who combed my hair when I was a child. I spent a lot of time sitting in front of and between my grandmother's legs, or those of other relatives, to get my hair oiled with Dax hair oil, combed, and styled. I mastered the *combing out the tangles look and tears*, especially after it was washed—this involved a lot of bawling and anguished facial expressions. But when it was finally styled in corn/cane rows, chiney bumps, as we called them (Bantu/Zulu/Nubian knots), plaits with bubbles, or another Caribbean style, I felt the *just got my hair styled* satisfaction. Of course, we have a lot more products now that help us style our natural hair much easier.

I felt honoured to comb my grandmother's hair. It was still natural—I don't think she ever relaxed it. I was worried about hurting her though, so I combed slowly and gently. She promptly stopped me.

"Girl, rake the hair! Rake the hair!"

She was telling me not to be gentle with her—to comb out the tangles. I reluctantly combed it a little harder, while still trying to be gentle. Her hair didn't have any tangles, though, so it was easier to comb than I expected.

As a child, I admired my grandmother's hair and wanted my hair to look like hers. When I asked her what she did to make her hair grow, she told me her banana tree ritual.

"Jacqueline, when I comb my hair, I roll the hair that comes out it into a ball. Then I shove it into the space between the base of the leaf and the trunk of the banana tree."

"This is what made your hair grow, Mama?"

"Yes."

I don't know if she later took a leaf from the banana tree and used it to make a treatment for her hair. It was another one of her quirky beliefs, likely passed down from our ancestors—for example, if you don't dispose of your hair properly, someone could get a hold of it and use it to work obeah against you. I had to test it, of course.

"I'll try the next time I comb my hair, Mama."

Every time she or I combed my hair, I went to the banana tree with my watt of hair and pushed it in. I checked my hair growth each day, or when I remembered, and waited and checked and waited and checked. Nothing happened. It didn't work for me. But we were far away from any banana trees, so my grandmother would have to settle for her wad of hair ending up in a less exotic place.

I didn't comb her hair on our next visit to the hospital. Instead, I sat at her bed watching her sleep soundly. As I looked at her small frame, sunken eyes and cheeks, I sensed that angels were standing by. I felt so sad that I started crying loudly, interrupting her tranquillity and forcing her to open her eyes. Apparently, I wasn't supposed to let her see me cry.

"Jacqueline [she didn't shorten my name], don't worry, everything's going to be alright," she whispered. "Everything's going to be alright."

She closed her eyes and sunk back into the deep stillness that she was enjoying.

That's the last thing she's going to say, I thought and said out loud. My mother and aunt, who were also in the room, didn't obey the no crying rule. In a few minutes, a nurse came and ushered us out of the room. It was the medical staff's instructions for us to keep our tears to ourselves, which the nurse also gently reminded us to do. We could cry all we wanted in the hallway.

They hadn't told her that she was dying, which is why we weren't supposed to cry in front of her. I'd never heard of a protocol like that; I'd want to know that I was dying. I think she knew, though—we know ourselves—and she had said goodbye to us in her own way.

Soon, it was our turn to say our final goodbyes. One or two mornings later, the hospital staff called to tell us to come quickly, for my grandmother's death was near. We scrambled to get dressed, and my mother, aunt, older cousin and I arrived at the hospital just in time.

My grandmother was unconscious, her breathing was irregular; she seemed to gasp, sometimes. Once again, we sat around her bedside. We watched as her breathing slowed. It slowed even more and she seemed to grimace, as if in pain—then she exhaled. I watched to see if her chest would rise and fall again, if she'd inhale once again…but she didn't. She was gone.

I wondered what she experienced as she took her last breath; I wondered this, but I didn't cry—I followed the no crying instructions from the nurses, finally! But it was because I'd already accepted her passing. I felt sad but was at peace. I don't remember her complaining of any pain before she died, but if she suffered at all, I felt comfort in the fact that it was over.

As my mother, aunt, cousin, and I sat with my grandmother, loud noises interrupted our quiet reflection. Some relatives who were in the hallway outside her room were upset and needed to be consoled, as they didn't make it on time to say goodbye.

• • •

The crying and consoling continued at my aunt's house, the meeting hub for relatives before and after my grandmother passed. It was a house with a long hallway at the entrance, with rooms on the first floor and additional rooms on the upper floor. Many relatives were packed in like sardines in the hallway and in just about every room. You couldn't move without touching someone as you passed them. People were drinking, laughing, crying, and telling stories about when my grandmother visited them the night before she died.

"Last night, my television fell over from its stand and dropped in an upright position. I knew it was her visiting me to say goodbye," one person said.

"I saw her walking in the house in a long, white nightgown," said another.

These stories were similar to the jumbie stories people told us when we were children. They were more funny than scary though. I was glad that I only experienced a restless night of sleep, before she passed.

My aunt planned my grandmother's funeral, with help from relatives. In the meantime, we visited her in the funeral home—my first experience with one. I was in awe of how professional and sensitive the funeral home staff were—how quietly they spoke, how attentive they were to our needs and questions. My grandmother was in the same large room each time we visited, which created the illusion that it was her private room. She would have appreciated this because when we were children, she taught us to be respectful of the deceased as they took their final journey.

We lived on a hill in Harris, so we could see funeral processions going up St. George's hill in the distance. During the procession, my grandmother insisted that there were certain things we couldn't do.

"Jacqueline, don't sweep the floor when you see a funeral procession."

"Yes, Mama."

"Jacqueline, stop and walk backwards."

"Yes, Mama."

"Don't point, either!"

These actions were considered disrespectful of the dead, and she believed that bad things could happen to us if we did them. It was her turn to get respect as she took her final journey.

Her funeral was the first one that I'd attended since leaving Montserrat. I was glad that no one lifted children or young people over the casket; I was too big at that point anyway. It was an emotional event, but I didn't cry and hadn't done so since crying at the hospital. I was still at peace with her passing because my grandmother had told me that everything was going to be alright. To me, it meant that even though I didn't have control over the situation, I should be optimistic I'd get through it. Like most grandmothers do for their grandchildren, she had a way of helping me feel anchored in the middle of a storm. Not only did I believe her then, but I adopted her words and they helped to make me feel anchored through other difficult situations. I experienced one of them when I was in my early twenties, a few years after her death, when a plane in which I was flying had to make an emergency landing.

• • •

It happened when I was on my way to Uganda with colleagues from the church I attended (Love and Faith World Outreach Ministries—a church with a Black pastor who reminded me of Prince). We had connecting flights, and the first leg was from Toronto to London. As we were about to cross the Atlantic Ocean, the pilot made an announcement.

"Ladies and gentlemen, this is your captain speaking," he said, with a distinct British accent that was very comforting. "We seemed to have lost an engine," he continued in his matter-of-fact voice.

What? Comfort quickly turned to concern as we listened intently.

"It could turn out to be a bit embarrassing if we continued to cross the Atlantic, so we're going to make an emergency landing in New York."

The pilot's dry sense of humour and reassuring voice cut the tension. So instead of panicking, we chuckled nervously and commented on his use of the word "embarrassing" to describe a potential disaster. I'd never experienced an emergency landing, so my imagination didn't run wild about landing scenarios, but I was also channelling my grandmother.

Jacqueline, everything's going to be alright.

Thankfully, we landed safely in New York and the airline put us up in a hotel. The next day, we successfully crossed the Atlantic and arrived in England.

• • •

At my grandmother's funeral, the different ways in which people handle grief were on full display. Those of Caribbean origin have very expressive grieving rituals—we let it all out and inadvertently provide comic relief. Some relatives couldn't stop crying in dramatic form; some broke down in the church, and others at the grave. One wanted to jump in the grave.

"I'm coming! I'm coming! [into the grave] Somebody hold me back!"

The relative was a healthy size, so I'm not sure how we would have held them back. Plus, if they really wanted to jump in, who could have stopped them? Although not outwardly obvious, I was being thoroughly entertained. I wasn't pointing or sweeping or doing other things that my grandmother told me not to do during funeral processions; maybe she wouldn't have been disappointed that I was deriving some joy from my relatives' pain. It all helped to ease the feeling of tremendous loss of my dear grandmother—the person who raised me during most of my formative years and with whom I had a strong bond. Home, in Montserrat, wasn't going to be the same without her.

They finished lowering Mama into the ground (without our relative, thankfully!) as we sang some of her favourite hymns, like "Nearer my God to Thee."

21

A Big Move

I arrived at Mercury Youth Services (now Turning Point Youth Services) in Toronto to speak with a counsellor about my home situation about a month after my grandmother's funeral. Things were still tense at home, and I was even more determined to find a way out after getting a jolt of reassurance from my grandmother's words. I was even more confident that everything would work out.

There were no cell phones back then, so I'd written the details of my situation on paper. I was worried that I'd forget things, when speaking with the counsellor—it happened sometimes when I was nervous.

I sat in a room, nervously tapping my toes, paper in hand, ready to bare my soul. I waited for the counsellor, who would be the lucky recipient of my tidal wave of words and emotions. When the door finally squeaked open, a male counsellor walked in. As he settled into his seat, I got ready to start. I opened my mouth, expecting the words to come rushing out, but the tidal wave started with tears only. My words were left behind in the first wave; perhaps they'd surface in the next wave.

They didn't. He was getting hammered with tears. *Why was I crying? Why wasn't my mouth working? I was nervous, but I had my paper. Okay…I'll find the words on my paper.*

As my mind was racing to figure out how to get the trapped words to come ashore, the counsellor got up to leave. It was as if he was swept back by an unexpected force.

Wait! I can tell you my story! I have my paper. Wait!

But he was gone, almost as quickly as he came in, as if swept away by my tears. I was left to tap my toes again.

The door finally squeaked open again; this time, a female counsellor walked in. It was as if the male counsellor had gone out of the room, made sure he was alone, did a spin, and with a flash of light, had transformed into Wonder Woman.

Will she be able to withstand the waves? I wondered. *Will she get things under control with her golden lasso of truth?*

The counsellor pulled up next to me, and I started again. The waves of tears continued, but this time my words finally surfaced. She didn't get up to leave, so she wasn't being pushed back by them. She was the breakwater, withstanding the relentless pounding of words and emotions. It was as if she used her Wonder Woman-silver bracelets to block the blows that pelted her like bullets. Not long after she came into the room, the strong waves of emotions abated. Before I knew it, the cleanup was in full operation as the counsellor thanked me for sharing my story so candidly and gave me some guidance and instructions for next steps.

"I've scheduled an appointment for you with an immigration officer."

"Okay, thank you."

"You'll need to take your passport and school report card with you. Please call or come by anytime, if you need to talk."

"Yes, I will."

It was just like Wonder Woman to know exactly what to do and quickly save the day.

I headed to my appointment with the immigration officer. I spared her the tidal wave experience; the counsellor at Mercury Youth Services had borne the brunt of it and the sea was much calmer now, if you will.

This immigration officer, like the counsellors, was white, but she didn't fit the stern, nicely-dressed white man stereotype.

"Jacqueline, you seem like a mature 16-year-old and you're doing well in school, so I'm going to help you."

"Thank you."

First, she submitted a request to break my mother's sponsorship so that I could be responsible for myself. Then, she connected me with Social Services. Later, a woman with whom I met at Social Services explained that I could live on my own or with a roommate, and she could help me find a place if needed. Once I provided my new address, I would start receiving monthly student welfare checks that would be enough for rent, food, transportation, and other basic necessities. The support would be provided until I graduated high school, after which I'd need to apply for a student loan for post-secondary education and living expenses.

It struck me that complete strangers had taken the time to hear and help me. They gave me the gift of feeling that I could take control of my situation and determine its outcome. It was empowering. They were all Wonder Women—not that Wonder Men couldn't have helped; it's just that I needed Wonder Women, at the time. I think the male counsellor I first saw at Mercury recognized that and was wise to adjust accordingly.

• • •

I also needed to adjust to taking responsibility for myself. I would start with securing a roommate. One of my friends knew someone who had a small apartment and was looking for one. She was a few years older than me, but, after meeting and clicking with her, we agreed to be roommates and the move-out countdown began.

On the day I prepared to leave the apartment, my mother called a friend for reinforcement. Earlier that same week, she had seen my packed suitcase and found the paper on which I'd written information, to facilitate my talk with the counsellor. She was hit with the tidal wave of written words, but spared the tears. They had long dried up, perhaps, but I was glad she now had a glimpse of how I felt. I also hadn't told her that I'd met with key people to get help, or my plans to move out, but she must have sensed that I was going somewhere, maybe on a trip, as she hid my passport. She reiterated her warning and was likely hoping that this time it would scare me straight.

"I'm going to send you back to Montserrat!"

She probably felt the exhaustion you might feel when a situation was out of control. I can't imagine what she experienced, wondering where her child was going and for how long, and whether she was going to be safe. I'm certain that I caused her some sleepless nights and possibly some premature grey hair.

I likely didn't sleep either, the night before I left. But I felt fully awake as I pulled my suitcase down the hallway of our apartment unit. Its wheels clanked loudly on the parquet floor as I headed to the front door. Seeing that I was about to leave the apartment, my mother insisted that I speak to the friend that she'd called. It may have been her last-ditch attempt to get someone to talk some sense into me. I was more like her than she probably imagined; she, too, left home at a relatively young age to come to Canada. Reluctantly, I took the phone and listened as her friend told me how scary the world was.

"Where are you going? Do you know all the bad things that can happen to you out there?"

Silence.

I was more confident in my decision and more prepared to go, "out there" than they realized, but I listened politely. I don't think they understood that I wasn't planning to come back home.

The friend stopped talking when she was satisfied that she had put the fear of God in me.

"Thank you," I said, and gave the phone back to my mother.

It was remarkable how little fear I felt, as I walked back to the front door, opened it, and walked out. What I did feel was that I had agency over my life. I was confident that things would work out. As my grandmother would have said: "Jacqueline, everything's going to be alright."

My friends Mitsy, Michelle, and Lav joined me when I got downstairs. We travelled for about three kilometres to my new address. We sang songs, as the wheels of my suitcase clanked loudly on the hard sidewalk pavement, almost keeping time for us, like a metronome.

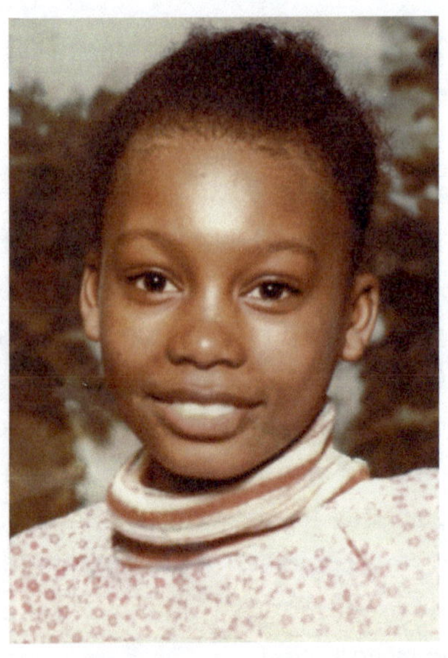

This is me in Grade 5, my first Picture Day experience. I had on the dress that I wore from Montserrat, with a turtle neck underneath.

Here, I was in Grade 7 or 8 in the school yard, at Donview Heights Junior High School.

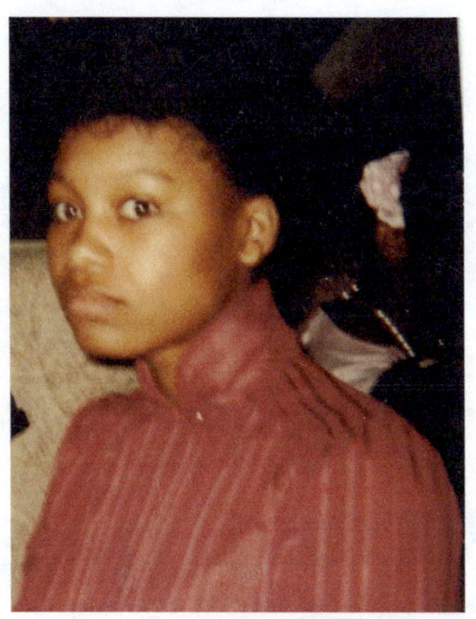

Here, I was 14 or 15, at a church banquet.
This picture probably reflects my general mood at that time.

Here I am in Grade 10, at our high school fashion show,
modelling an outfit that I made in Family Studies.

Here I am in Grade 11 at our high school fashion show, modelling another outfit that I made in Family Studies.

Part 3

Building Up and Tearing Down

22

On My Own

"Love your neighbour as yourself" (Matthew 22:39) is one of my favourite scriptures. To me, it implies that we all love ourselves, and I would argue that it's impossible to hate yourself. The challenge is to love others the same way that you love yourself—to consider how your actions impact others and whether they are in the best interest of yourself, others, and society at large. It's not always easy to do and entails a lifetime of actions, missteps, adjustments, and growth.

When I moved out at 16 years old, I wasn't focused on how my actions impacted others, like my mother. My own well-being was my priority. I continued to attend the same church for a short time, so my mother had confirmation that I was alive and well. It was a large church, so I could avoid speaking with her, except for a few times when she ran into me and expressed her disappointment about me moving out. My father, on the other hand, had no idea what had transpired. I didn't tell him about my home situation; I hadn't spoken to him since coming to Canada. I hadn't had to depend on him in the past, so I didn't consider asking him for help. I also didn't tell him that I was living on my own until a couple of years later. I worried he might think that I wasn't capable of being on my own or appreciate all the work that I'd done to prepare. But I planned to visit him in Montserrat when I was more settled and tell him all about it.

In the meantime, being on my own started well. I'll show you around my new home.

You're walking through the door of my apartment with me. We'll enter the front area with the living room straight ahead. Turning right takes you to the bathroom and then the bedroom. Turning left takes you through a doorway and into the kitchen, and another doorway from the kitchen takes you to the dining room. From there, walk a couple of steps into the living room. It was sparsely furnished with wicker furniture, and we had a beautiful budgie that was chirpy and messy. We had a nice bedroom set and a comfortable bed. More accurately, my new roommate had furnished it long before I arrived and graciously shared with me.

I didn't have all the details worked out when I started working on a long-term plan at 13—with whom I was going to live and where…what furniture I would buy…how much money I would need...My plan lacked the sophistication that comes with age and experience. But I had a big dose of courage, partly from the fact that I thought I was grown at 13 years old; I thought that I knew a lot more than my mother—that natural struggle with wanting to be an adult but not having a clue what it entails. That kind of delusional thinking probably contributed to my confidence.

Ultimately, I got a lot of help. Contacting immigration was an important step in setting me on the right path, and things fell into place afterwards. Often, success comes with taking a step in the direction in which you want to go, bravely following the path enfolding before you, connecting with the key people who can help you achieve your goals, and adjusting when things don't unfold as expected.

As Social Services promised, I received my first monthly check. I was excited to see it and could pay my half of the rent, buy groceries, and purchase a bus pass with it. Still, I quickly realized that I had to budget carefully; I didn't have a lot of money for things like clothes and shoes, and even groceries, sometimes. That wasn't necessarily a bad thing as it motivated me to set another goal—work hard to achieve financial independence, as soon as possible.

So, I started selling Avon and working at the McDonald's nearby. With Avon, it was about connecting with people, sales and marketing skills, and a lot of patience when I didn't sell as much as I wanted to. With McDonald's, I learned customer service and built on the strong work ethic that my grandmother and mother instilled in me. I still remember the mottos the managers drilled into us, stances shared by many service organizations: "The customer is always right!" and "If you have time to lean, you have time to clean!" I'd throw on my "Welcome to McDonald's" persona and work my butt off. Depending on how much additional income I earned, Social Services would reduce my next month's check. Sometimes, I had to find creative and cost-effective ways to make ends meet, like getting a seamstress at my church to make some of my clothes and getting free food from McDonald's.

The last shift of the day entailed throwing out unsold prepared food and prepping the store for the next day. Globally, it's astounding how much food gets tossed out. If all that food was redistributed, we could probably feed every hungry person on the planet and help the climate by reducing the greenhouse gases from rotting food. It wouldn't solve all the issues, but it would help.

I remember the first time I worked the last shift and heard my colleague say: "Okay Jackie [I started using the shortened version of my name], we're going to throw out the prepared food that we didn't sell."

"What? Why are we doing that? I'm taking some home."

I packed our freezer at home with hamburgers, Big Macs, and more and had food to eat when I was low on money. I could've run my own McDonald's franchise out of that freezer. Well, maybe not, but I could at least share some with my friends, if they didn't mind eating a not-so-fresh burger—most of them minded, though.

"Yuck! How can you eat this?" they'd ask. "It's soggy and stale!"

Who wouldn't prefer a fresh burger? But when you have a tight budget, you learn not to mind; you learn to like the night shift.

One day, I met a boy while working a day shift. I wasn't popular with boys, probably because I was socially awkward with them and very focused on church. I was also unusually tall, which most boys didn't appreciate back then. Many girls are taller now. As a Gen Xer, I remember when I first started seeing Millennials in the mall and my surprise at how many girls were over six feet tall. I started feeling short at 5'10"/1.78m.

But back to my boys' woes. I'd seen a couple of boys in elementary school, with nice afros. I liked them, but they weren't my friends, and they barely spoke to me. I'm not sure why I liked boys with afros, like the boy who told me to keep my foolishness to myself, back in Montserrat. Maybe it was because my mother had an afro in her pictures. There were boys that I thought were cute in junior high, too, but they didn't interact with me. Surprisingly, the boy that I met at McDonald's liked me, and other boys were noticing me too; maybe I exuded more confidence being on my own.

I saw him as I was wrapping up work at the front of the store. We had an internal code that we called out when we saw someone that we liked. I called it out to my co-workers. They understood it to mean that there was a good-looking guy in the line. We laughed discreetly, as we did when we heard the code. I'd forgotten about him when I went to the back of the store, to prepare to go home. When I came back to the front to head out, I was surprised that he was waiting there.

"Hello, Jackie. Do you remember me?"

"Nope. I don't."

"I play basketball sometimes at the court at your friend's apartment."

"Oh…"

I vaguely remembered seeing him from a distance but had never spoken to him and didn't know who he was. He seemed nice so we exchanged numbers and dated for a couple of months. It was fun at first, and he visited my church a few times, but we eventually parted ways—our interests in church were too different.

I wasn't having any success with relationships, but work and school were going well, although I'd soon hit a snag. When a social worker from Social Services visited (maybe monthly), I'd give him an update on things. I sensed that the main purpose of his visits was to observe and get an update on my living situation and activities. Social Services would have wanted to make sure that I wasn't taking advantage of the system, of hard-earned tax payer dollars. It made sense to me. But if I could've changed things, I would've made visits a mix of support (coaching and counselling) and accountability. I'm not sure if more support would have changed my disappointing last year of high school, though.

• • •

I transitioned from Victoria Park to Georges Vanier High School, as it had a semester model. This would allow me to finish school in the first semester and move on to post-secondary education;

I wanted to transition off student welfare and be more self-sufficient. It wasn't a bad strategy, but I'd soon realize a flaw in my planning. So far, my one big plan to move out had worked so I was confident that subsequent plans would also work. I hadn't yet been stung by the pain of failure so I didn't recognize the need for a contingency plan to handle things that could go wrong—it was only a matter of time before something went wrong.

I failed chemistry. It was the first course that I'd failed, but, more importantly, I needed it to graduate. I was devastated. I had probably skipped one too many classes. I thought I was smart enough to juggle school and work and skip some classes and still do well. I didn't realize then that there were subjects that were naturally easy for me (language studies, social and environmental studies, and the arts) and others that weren't, that I needed to put more effort into (math and science). I thought it would be painful to do another semester for one course, so I didn't. That was a mistake, but I quickly decided on next steps and moved forward.

A friend told me about a short program at Career Canada College that appealed to me, so I got a student loan, transitioned off student welfare, and by 19 years old, I completed a Medical Office and Laboratory Assistant Diploma. I planned to continue my education later.

In the meantime, I was happy to get a better paying job and work towards my financial goals. I worked in various labs doing phlebotomy, electrocardiograms (ECGs), etc., and started paying off my student loan.

23
Reconciliations

When I was 19 or 20 years old, a mutual friend of mine and my mother told me that my mother was sick. She had already visited my mother and planned to visit her again. One day when I was driving with her, she told me that she needed to pick up something at my mother's apartment.

"Jackie, you should come with me to see your mother."

"No...I'll wait in the car. I don't want to go, and, besides, I don't think my mother even wants to see me."

"Well, just come and see how things go. I'll be there, too. I can do the talking."

"I don't think it's a good idea, but...okay."

I liked my old neighbourhood; being there made me feel nostalgic. I hadn't returned home since leaving at 16, nor spoken with my mother and stepfather other than a couple of times when I ran into my mother at my previous church. I'd spent my childhood dreaming of going "away" to see her; I still have at least one of the letters that I wrote to her when I was seven or eight years old, reminding her to "send for me." My mother had saved a few of them for me. But, ironically, after spending the first ten years of my life wanting to get to my mother, I spent most of the next ten years moving away.

I don't think that I thought coming to Canada would make me happier, but it's natural for children to want to be with their parents or at least know who they are. I knew instinctively that external sources (things and people) don't bring happiness, so when things didn't work out, I found a solution that worked for me. But things and people matter, too, because everything and everyone are connected and dependent.

Reluctantly, I went to see my mother with our mutual friend. As we walked into her room, I could see that she was lying down and didn't look well.

"Hello, mom."

"Hello."

That was the extent of our exchange; it was very awkward and got worse when my friend quickly left the room after saying a few things to my mother. I realized then that she'd set me up. My friend had been doing all the talking, and now I was forced to say something. I could tell that my mother wasn't happy with me as she was very serious and wasn't talkative. I felt like that little child who couldn't find the words to say. I thought any nice words would seem disingenuous as our relationship was strained and any harsh words would be inappropriate as my mother was sick. She said a few things to me about not understanding why I moved out and that nobody told me to, and after sitting in awkward silence, I stood up.

"Okay, I'm leaving now." With that, I quickly left her room to avoid the lecture.

A few months later, my mother gave birth to my brother, Everton; her sickness was pregnancy-related. I went back to the apartment to see him and was quite surprised when I first saw him; I was expecting to see a small baby but he wasn't small at all.

"Wow, he's so big! How much does he weigh?"

"Well, he was ten pounds at birth."

"And did you say that you delivered him without any anaesthesia?"

"Yes, I delivered all of you without anaesthesia."

"That's incredible. I don't think I have the same high tolerance for pain."

Everton made it easy for me to find something to talk to my mother about; I was fascinated with the fact that he looked more like a toddler, ready to play ball. I'd go back to see him again, and my other two siblings, too, and before long, I was enjoying dinner and laughs. But my mother and I didn't discuss why I moved out. I don't think either of us were ready to have the conversation.

A couple of years after my brother was born, my mother gave birth to my sister Annemarie, who became another reason for me to keep visiting. I was still not fond of my stepfather, but we managed to be civil—meaning, I no longer had a reason to fight with him, nor he with me, but we still barely spoke to each other.

It's interesting that even though we all attended church, we were all still learning how to navigate relationships; it's that ongoing process of actions, missteps, adjustments, and growth. I had moved from my mother's church and even started working full-time at my church as a minister when I was about 21 years old. But I was still learning how to navigate relationships. I wasn't doing well with achieving my goal of financial independence, either; I didn't get paid very much working as a minister. I couldn't afford to do things of interest like visit my home in Montserrat.

But in 1988, the year before Hurricane Hugo wreaked havoc on Montserrat and other islands, unexpectedly, I got an opportunity to travel to countries in Africa with church colleagues; someone had deferred their visit, allowing me to go instead.

• • •

It was the same trip in which the pilot had to make an emergency landing in New York because we'd lost one of the engines. We were put up in New York, and then London, England, before heading to South Africa. I was excited to land on the continent of Africa, for the first time; like many others of African descent, I learned about where my ancestors originated, and their journey across the ocean. I wanted to connect to the motherland I'd been removed from by a combination of circumstances and time. For many, colonialism ensured we accepted England as our mother land, but not Africa—like accepting our adoptive but not our biological parent. In fact, I don't see any symbols of Africa on Montserrat's flag, only British and Irish elements. But, like many adopted children, we want to know where we're from.

We visited Uganda, which was still recovering from decades of dictator rule, then Zimbabwe, with its natural beauty. We continued on to Swaziland, where we learned about the royal family. By the end of our six-week stay, visiting ministers and churches, I left with a greater appreciation for who I am, my connection to my ancestors, and the influence of African history and culture on the Caribbean, and other parts of the world.

I saw both poverty and wealth, but the people that we met were spiritual, creative, strong, regal, and had a surety and sense of belonging rooted in a strong culture and identity. The way they danced—that rolling of the hips, sometimes one hip at a time with pauses and dips for emphasis…the way they expressed themselves, as well as some of their music—sounds that were similar to reggae and calypso, against the beat of African drums and other instruments…the food and customs—delicious matoke, a type of banana in Uganda, and Nile perch...the way they toiled and thrived and carried themselves with grace...their wisdom and wit...it was all very familiar and similar to Caribbean customs. There were times when it felt like I was in the Caribbean. And even though there was no physical place there that I could call home, it was still like returning home after being away on a long journey, across the ocean and across time.

24

Bells and Bonnets

When I returned from my visit abroad, I started working at the Scarborough General Hospital processing and analyzing medical records—a job that helped me achieve more financial independence and stability. I also continued to be active in church, where we learned the importance of writing and realizing our vision. Some people had visions that included how their future family would look (kind of like vision boards). Sometimes, people got a little carried away, though. Their vision statement included the name of their spouse, but if it wasn't reciprocated, well, that was a problem—a possible "Obeah Wedding Song" scenario. The "name it and claim it" prosperity gospel approach, gone too far.

Despite some missteps, many were successful with getting married and having children, and some are still married today. I met someone who was hard-working and consistent with his commitments; it seemed like a good idea, at the time, to follow suit and also get married, even though we hadn't known each other for a long time. So, at 24 years old, I got married.

• • •

There were about 100 people at my wedding, which had African and European themes. I wore a traditional ruffled wedding gown with a presentation bouquet of Cali lilies. I also had an African reception outfit but didn't end up changing. The bridesmaids wore dresses made from pseudo-African print (they hated them!) and the groom and groomsmen wore suits, with hats that incorporated an African theme.

It was important for me that my father participate in my wedding. I hadn't seen him since immigrating to Canada 14 years earlier; I hadn't returned to Montserrat to see him and other relatives and friends. But I established contact with him by phone around 19 years old and continued to speak with him occasionally. In my mid-twenties, I was ready to get married and shared my plans with him by phone.

"Dad, will you come to my wedding and give me away?"

I followed a few antiquated traditions like this one, but adopted my own meaning, versus the original meaning of a father giving his property to another man.

"Jacqueline, nothing will stop me from coming."

I was delighted with seeing him after so long as we reunited and walked proudly down the aisle together. I'd come a long way since the strange sensations that I felt when I first met him at eight years old, on the side of the road in Mos Ghaut. We floated down the aisle, as we did back then, but this time I had a quiet knowing of who he was, of who I was—it was father and daughter sharing a moment.

My mother and stepfather walked down the aisle, too, as part of the ceremony—my brother Everton and sister Annemarie were ring bearer and flower girl, respectively. My other sisters, Dionne and Maxine, were also part of the wedding activities, along with some of my friends—Shelly, Justice, Natalie, Thecla, and Ann. And my friend Mitsy, whom I met in junior high school, graced us by singing a couple of songs. My cousin Olivene, who had immigrated to Canada, was also part of the wedding. My eldest brother Sam attended—I'd met him a few years earlier when he visited me in Canada—and my paternal grandmother (Granny Katie), Aunt Irene, and Cousins Ingrid and Ida also attended; I met them for the first time.

Other than some disagreements with my spouse about silly things I can't even remember, the wedding went well and I settled into married life. A few months later, I was surprised when my body felt different. A pregnancy test lit up immediately, confirming my pregnancy. I was scared and confused but quickly shifted to prenatal care and planning. I had a moment of shock when I learned a few weeks later that I was pregnant with twins.

My pregnancy went relatively well, and on a Sunday evening in July, as I settled into bed, I felt what I thought were Braxton Hicks (false labour contractions). But the frequency and intensity were different.

"I think I might be in labour," I calmly said to my husband.

He called the hospital and they told him to bring me in. Hearing that it was time for the twins to be delivered, I had a complete meltdown. It was two weeks before the scheduled C-section date.

What? I'm not ready! I thought.

"I don't want to go. I've changed my mind," I wailed.

He called my mother and asked her to convince me to leave the house.

"You have to go now," my mother insisted.

"I don't want to go!"

"I'll meet you there, don't worry," she said, almost channelling my grandmother.

A few hours later, I delivered my children via Caesarean Section—my son, Lemuel was the smaller twin at 6lbs 1oz/2760g, and my daughter Gabrielle was 7lbs 14oz/3580g. They were both beautiful and weighed more than the average weight of 5.5lbs/2495g for twins.

"You let your brother take all the hair?" I asked and told my daughter simultaneously. It's a Caribbean thing to want your girl to have more hair than your boy. I envisioned styling her hair the way my grandmother styled my hair when I was a child—corn/cane rows, chiney bumps, plaits with bubbles. I didn't see until later that she had more hair in the back and sides. I'd have something to work with after all.

Taking care of twins was a lot of work, but I managed by using a tip that I got from someone who had twins—put them on the same schedule. Feed, bathe, put them to sleep at the same time; rest while they rest. I'd repeat most of those activities several times a day, so a schedule was going to be key to keeping my sanity. But I'd also concluded that two children, rather than the four that I'd planned to have, was more than enough.

25

Disruptions and Eruptions

As with more than 50% of marriages in North America, mine bit the dust a few years after I got married. From my perspective, we were on different pages, in terms of goals and beliefs. My beliefs were more liberal; I wanted to continue to work outside of the home to maintain my employability and independence. I was fine with celebrating events like Halloween for the sake of the children, though I also disliked the emphasis on death and gore. I was also becoming less interested in the church we attended. After a few years of trying to make things work, countless conflicts, and one major blow-up, we parted ways. Based on the results of my last year of high school, evidently, I had a lot to learn about chemistry.

I have great admiration for my friends and colleagues who have maintained strong relationships, though.

• • •

While my attention was focused on my marital problems, something happening about 6,000 km away caught my attention: Montserrat was in turmoil.

I'd tried to avoid getting sent back there when I moved out at 16 years old and had spent the next few years establishing myself. Although I planned to return home one day, I hadn't made it a priority. In the meantime, a catastrophe was unfolding there.

It was 1995, and my children were toddlers, so I was quite busy and didn't always listen to the news. I think it was my mother who first told me about Montserrat's Soufrière Hills volcano.

"Jackie, the volcano in Montserrat erupted. I think it's Chances Peak."

The volcano had erupted on July 18, 1995, after being dormant for almost 400 years. It started small, venting steam, generating earthquakes, and then increased its activities.

"What? Chances Peak is a dormant volcano?"

I was a little confused as I'd never thought of the mountain as a sleeping volcano. Chances Peak is one of the mountains in the Soufrière Hills Mountain range and the one with which I was most familiar as it was near my house; the one that was like a picture on a wall I passed every day and barely noticed.

But it had my attention now. The volcano continued its activities into 1996. I tuned into the news, only to hear heart-wrenching stories, Montserratians running from places like Plymouth to the north of the island, even to other islands. Then they'd return, thinking that the volcano had settled down, but it was quietly building up material at its peak for the next round.

My mother told me that our relatives were okay. My father left Montserrat for a nearby island soon after the eruptions started; he was also okay. Some of my relatives who were "away" and had properties near Plymouth heard about damages to them. Some of the buildings, houses, roads and cars were covered in ashes; I was surprised to see pictures and videos of people shovelling ashes and brushing it off cars. It reminded me of shovelling after a relentless snowfall. But the relatively small volume of snowfalls that I've experienced over the years, and even heavy packing snow, couldn't compare to dense volcanic material which irritated your skin, got into your pores and lungs.

I watched and listened to the news as the volcanic activities continued and people had to be evacuated again. I heard someone say, "This is my home, I'm not leaving!" Some chose to stay on Montserrat, but as the eruptions increased and intensified, others emigrated to England and other countries. I was relieved when my mother confirmed that our relatives made it out safely. Of those who stayed, several risked their lives by going back into the areas that were considered dangerous and off limits (Farms, Harris, Farrels, Windy Hill, Streathams, and other areas). They went to check their properties and even work on their lands, and it is possible that some had never left.

In 1997, I'd left my marriage and had moved with my children into an apartment in Markham, Ontario. Then, sadly, that same year in June 1997, my mother gave me some shocking news.

"Jackie, our neighbour from Harris died in the latest eruption."

"No! How?"

"She went back to Harris to get belongings and the volcano erupted while she was still there. She didn't make it out."

"No! Oh my God!"

She was someone whom I knew very well. I felt so sad when I heard the news about her and the 18 other people who were also killed in the same eruption; they, too, were in the danger zone. It was painful and difficult to imagine people being overtaken by hot gases, boulders, lava, and ashes, let alone someone with whom I interacted regularly when I was a child. Others who survived spoke about struggling to breathe and see, when gases and ashes filled the air and darkened the skies. Some reported narrowly escaping and suffering serious burns. Many had to move in with friends and family or into temporary shelters, with little privacy or comfort. I wondered about the long-term impact of the trauma, injuries, poor air quality, and destruction.

By then, I, along with my mother and other relatives, had turned into "volcano experts." We were talking about tectonic plates, lava domes, and pyroclastic flows, as if they were a normal part of our vocabulary. We hoped that we had seen the worst of things.

But the volcano wasn't finished. Later that year, we heard the news that it extended its reach to the airport, nearby villages, and Plymouth, destroying them. I was awestruck when I saw pictures, including one showing a deep crevice that the volcano carved between Paradise and Harris along the main road and Mos Ghaut. It barely missed the Anglican church. Miraculously, most properties in Harris seemed to be unaffected—the Methodist church (rebuilt with concrete, after Hurricane Hugo destroyed it), police station, and other buildings and houses were still there. I was hopeful that Harris would be spared.

With the airport and Plymouth destroyed and the jetty in Plymouth damaged, tourism was severely impacted. Getting to and from Montserrat pre-eruption was never straightforward; the volcano exacerbated access issues. In addition, because the volcano eruptions had impacted agricultural lands and crops, roads, as well as homes and businesses, Montserrat's economy took a big hit. Ultimately, about two thirds of the island was evacuated and designated an exclusion zone. Approximately half the population left their homes and lives in Montserrat, and the future seemed bleak.

I was shocked and traumatized by the devastation but didn't fully comprehend the extent of the disaster or what Montserratians who were living through it endured. I'd never experienced an active volcano, nor considered that one could destroy our home. I always assumed home would be there when I was ready to return. Being away for such a long time had proven to have consequences that I had not imagined.

• • •

In 2005, things were looking up in Montserrat even though the volcano continued to be active. Things were looking up for me, too, even though some aspects of my life felt like an active volcano—disrupting and permanently destroying things, testing my resolve, forcing me along alternate paths while inspiring me to be innovative. I'd gone back to school and, after a few years of juggling school, work, taking care of my children, overcoming some fibroid-related health issues, financial challenges, and even dealing with the theft of my car, I'd graduated with a degree in Computer Science. I'd also gotten a better-paying job at the Canadian Institute for Health Information and continued to achieve and even surpass my financial goals. By following simple financial management principles (pay debts, increase savings, decrease spending, invest, give), I eventually achieved a socio-economic transformation. With gratitude for help that I'd received along the way, I could start to look up and ahead to establishing generational wealth, to contributing to addressing systemic wealth interruptions and a cycle of poverty.

Montserrat was also achieving some goals in the face of its natural and socio-political eruptions. Initially, Montserratians were not happy with the way the UK handled the crisis—the amount and timeliness of volcano-specific financial aid...funds for resettling in the UK and other places...plans to completely evacuate/

close the island...and more. But Montserrat's government used the funds to build a new airport to replace the Blackburne/W.H. Bramble Airport; The government also continued to implement other recovery efforts like building permanent houses for people who had to be resettled from areas that were evacuated. I was happy to hear about the progress and thankful that my village, although off limits, was still intact in 2005.

Things seemed to be settling down. But then the volcano did the unthinkable—in 2010, I got the news of a major eruption. This time, it completely buried the airport and surrounding areas. It also destroyed my village—homes, land, roads, buildings, animals, trees—just about everything.

"Oh my God. Harris was hit!" But I didn't know how bad it was.

It was difficult to look at some of the pictures posted online. I saw some of the Seventh Day Adventist church and the Harris Clinic. The walls and foundations were spared, but the roof, windows, doors, and anything combustible were destroyed. I also saw a picture of the Black Mango Tree near Brother Reiny's house. It was scorched, but a small part of its trunk was still there. I couldn't find pictures or videos that showed the full extent of the devastation, so I maintained a level of denial, wondering...

What else was spared in our village?

Was the house in which I lived still there? Most of it was spared during Hurricane Hugo, but would the volcano be as kind?

Maybe the veranda, though imperfect when I was a child, had withstood the relentless pounding from ashes and pyroclastic flows, at least.

Maybe ...just maybe, everything was going to be alright.

Here is my father walking with me down the aisle, at my wedding.

Here are my bridesmaids in the hideous outfits that I made them wear.
We were at the Guildwood Park and Gardens, Scarborough, Ontario.

Here I am with my mother and sister Dionne, at my wedding.

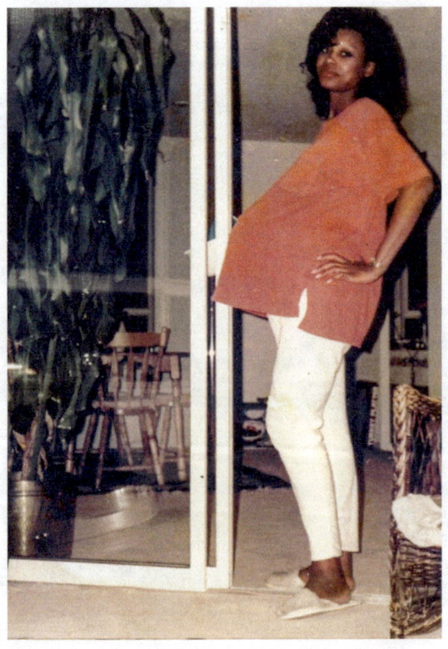

I took this picture two weeks before I delivered the twins. They were running out of room and I was physically uncomfortable.

Here are my children at five months.

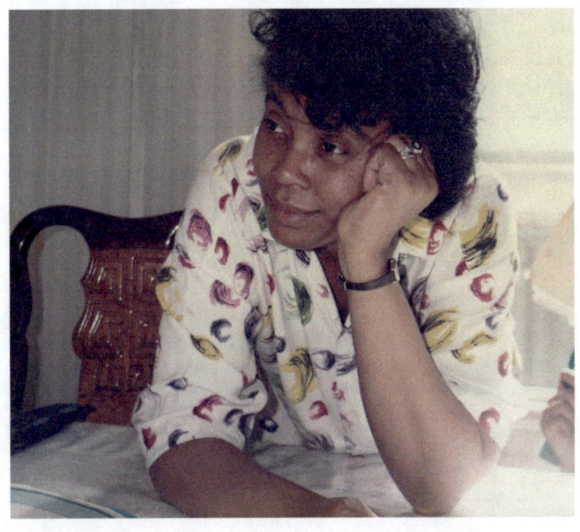

This is my mother, relaxing at her house.

Here I am with my children at my mother's house.

My children in elementary school.

My children at their elementary school graduation.

My children at their high school prom.

Me and my children. My son appreciated reaching my height, and eventually growing taller than me.

My father and eldest brother, Sam, at Sam's wedding.

My father, sister (Venerine) and my niece, at my brother Sam's wedding.

My paternal grandmother (Katie), aunt (Irene), sister (Mavis), niece (Zherine) and me, at my brother Sam's wedding.

My mother at my sister Dionne's wedding, in Jamaica.

My mother and all her children, and a few of her grandchildren, at a birthday party.

Part 4

Home

26

My Montserrat

By 2016, it had been 21 years since the volcano erupted and six years since the last major eruption—the one that destroyed my village. Montserratians from Harris and other areas who'd chosen to stay were settling into their new homes in the north. The government continued to rebuild and even lifted access restrictions to some areas. Some Montserratians pressed the government to free up land in safe parts of the exclusion zone, desperately needed for housing and agriculture; also, I know some who continue to patiently wait for their homes in the exclusion zone to be released for their use. Things seemed somewhat stable, so I decided that it was time, well past time, to finally return home. I made plans to visit Montserrat, with my children, who were in their mid-twenties by then.

As we descended into Antigua, I admired the vibrant colours of the Caribbean Sea. We'd be back in the air soon to complete our journey to Montserrat. *We were almost there! Almost home!* I looked forward to seeing what remained of my village. But my experience in Antigua would hint of the challenging road home.

Imagine you're at the airport with me in the departure area. We'll have to wait a while before boarding the plane to Montserrat.

"Hello," I said, approaching the counter, after someone finally called me. I knew from experience that I probably wasn't going to hear something good.

"Hello. I wanted to inform you that your plane was delayed on another island, due to an emergency."

Okay, that explained why the wait was starting to feel so long...

"Thanks for the update. When will the plane arrive?"

"I'm not sure, but you won't be able to fly to Montserrat this evening. The airport there is closed."

I was confused by this news, as she could probably tell from my knitted brows, squinted eyes, and head tilted to one side. *It was a few minutes before 6:00 p.m.—how could the airport be closed? Was there an emergency in Montserrat, too*?

"What do you mean the airport is closed?" I asked, incredulous.

"Well, the airport closes at 6:00 p.m. every day, so there's no way to get there by plane, until tomorrow."

"Really?"

I'd never heard of an airport closing so early. We learned later that it was from the volcanic ash remaining in the air, which, at night, impacted visibility for pilots. It was another way in which the volcano had added to existing challenges with accessing Montserrat.

Feeling disappointed, we spent the night in Antigua and returned to the airport early in the morning. You'll see that this time the plane was there, a nine-seater (including the pilot and co-pilot seats)—smaller than we imagined. It didn't fly at a high altitude, so we could clearly see the Caribbean Sea, glistening with hues of blues and greens. I was amused by my son, who prayed fervently to ease his fear of flying so close to the water. It distracted me from my feelings of claustrophobia in the small space.

We were only in the air for a few minutes when, through the wispy low hanging clouds, we saw the mountains.

"There it is!" I exclaimed.

It was Montserrat rising up in the distance—the Emerald Isle of the Caribbean—this tagline used to be followed by "The Land of Beautiful Women and Mountain Chicken" (frogs, which are a delicacy and can only be found on Montserrat and Dominica); the tag may have been dropped because the volcanic eruptions and other issues endangered the frogs—there is a project in place to restore the population.

I kept my eyes on the land as if it might disappear if I dared to look away. It was like a beacon, guiding us to its shores. As we got closer, we had a better view of the mountains, covered with blankets of green foliage, the vibrant green hills and the rugged coastline. *It was absolutely stunning!*

We didn't have a good view of the volcano as we flew in from the north, and there were clouds covering the volcano mountains in the south. What we could see were the roads, houses, and buildings carved into the terrain, like carefully placed components of a painting. One of them was the John A. Osborne Airport in Gerald's Village, which is where we touched down. It was named after Montserrat's Chief Minister (1978–1991 and 2001–2006) and was about the size of a large house, with a very long driveway. The runway is one of the shortest commercial runways in the world. It's not long enough to accommodate larger airplanes like the LIAT planes that used to land at the old airport. Montserratians have talked about building bigger.

• • •

Offboard, we'll take a moment to inhale the Montserrat air and feel grateful for arriving home safely. My son was grateful that his feet were finally on the ground; my daughter, too. I'd never been to this part of the island but it felt familiar—it felt like home.

We proceeded through immigration and collected our luggage (picture maneuvering in a large house—everything was a few feet away).

"I've returned home after 39 years and brought my children with me," I said to the immigration officer, who asked us the purpose of our visit.

"Welcome home! 39 years is a long time to stay away."

"Yes, I've been 'away' for a long time but I'm finally back and glad to be home."

As we chatted, he told me things in Montserrat were good and that he had multiple jobs but wasn't stressed at all. The slower pace was palpable as we interacted with him. Later, we travelled by taxi to the Tropical Mansions Suites hotel, located in Davy Hill; we arrived in less than ten minutes, a far cry from the traffic jams in Canada and other countries, which you typically won't experience in Montserrat. The Galloways, a Black Montserratian family, built the hotel to help bring tourists back to the island after the volcano eruption; it opened in 1999.

From the hotel, we seemed to be far from Harris, Plymouth, and the volcano. But I could see Little Bay, where the new capital of Montserrat was under construction. The National Museum of Montserrat, Marine Village, Little Bay Port, Montserrat Festival Village, the cricket field, the Public Market, and other establishments had already been constructed. It was nice to learn that specialists from Sprung Instant Structures Ltd., in Canada, assembled the external structure of the Montserrat Sports Arena and Sir George Martin built and gifted the Montserrat Cultural Centre to the island.

We went to the Cultural Centre to enjoy the Masquerade and other performances. My memories rushed back as I explained to my children about my terrifying childhood experiences with Masquerades and my greater appreciation for them as an adult. They are mesmerizing visual storytellers whose messages and movements reverberate in my innermost being. I've been brought to tears multiple times while watching their videos; I can see and feel my ancestors through them—I can see and feel their pain and triumph. I've learned that like Mountain Chicken, Montserrat Masquerades are in danger of extinction because those who practice it are getting older; younger people aren't as interested. But I'm glad that there is a focused effort to ensure that the skills and customs are passed on to the next generation.

We also went nearby to the Montserrat Festival Village. As we approached the entrance, I spotted my brother. I spent some weekends at his house when I was a child. The last time I saw him was when he visited me in Canada when I was about 20 years old. I wasn't able to connect with him before coming to Montserrat, so I'd planned to look him up. Given the size of the population—approximately 5,000 people at the time—I knew it would be easy. But I didn't expect it to happen on our first day. Walking right up to him, I tapped him on the shoulder.

"Hello, Silford!"

He looked puzzled and I could see the wheels turning.

"It's Jackie—your sister—and your niece and nephew!"

Shock. Confusion. It took him a minute to realize it was me.

"Jackie!? Jackie!?" he kept repeating as he hugged me and my children. "I can't believe it's you."

We reunited and then headed into the Montserrat Festival Village.

"Jackie!? Jackie!?" he repeated, again.

Come inside with me! We'll take in the surroundings as my brother recovers from shock.

I could see that Festival Village was comparable to Sturge Park with its nice, large stage and nearby cricket field. We enjoyed listening and dancing to soca/calypso music—"Bum Bum" was one of the hit songs that year. In fact, Montserratians seemed to be continuing all of our cultural celebrations, like the Carnival Parade, in which we participated, on another day—jamming from Carr's Bay to Little Bay…the Calypso Monarch and Festival Queen competitions…other Christmas Festival events…and other celebrations throughout the year. Like the example set by our ancestors, hard times can't stop us from celebrating our history and culture, even if we have to adapt and do so in new ways. We'd also added to our culture. For example, at about 6:00 a.m., or earlier, one morning, I was awoken by the sounds of a parade in which revellers had painted their bodies and were throwing colourful powder on each other as they jammed down Sweeney's Road; this is a Trinidadian custom.

At Festival Village, my brother enjoyed bush rum (basically, my grandmother's fever grass concoction spiked with rum), while we feasted on goat water and Johnny cakes. My daughter liked goat water, but my son wasn't keen on trying it. He eventually took a few sips, to avoid having to tell his grandmother that he didn't try Montserrat's national dish.

Plymouth and surrounding areas were beautiful back in the day, but Little Bay surpassed them with its modern layout, built using 21st century technology. It was a refreshing and beautiful new hub that we enjoyed before heading back to our hotel. There, we could also see Brades, the temporary location of government buildings, as well as houses, banks, and other businesses.

It was where we went the next day to exchange money and check my bank account that my aunt/sister told me about. She'd visited me in Canada a few years earlier and surprised me with a bank book. It was for an account that my grandmother opened for me when I was a child. It had a small balance and, other than interest, hadn't been active since 1977, the year I left Montserrat. It was like a clock that had stopped at the time of a life-changing event. All my activities on Montserrat came to a full stop then, but I was back to continue my journey—to create a new chapter in my story.

I expected to hear that the account was closed due to inactivity; that the funds were no longer accessible, or that they subtracted regular bank fees until there were no more funds. I was more curious than hopeful that it was still there and was pleasantly surprised when I heard the clerk tell me that it was, in fact, still there.

"Yes, it's here. It's dormant, though, so you can either activate or close it."

I felt an injection of hope as I activated the account and wrapped up at the bank. Then we went further up the hill to do more business and then back down the hill. In this beautiful and bustling area of Montserrat, also newly developed, many places were up or down a steep hill. Contrary to the look of discomfort on my face in a picture that my daughter snapped, I liked climbing hills. It might be the reason that I climbed the 1776 steps of the Canadian National (CN) Tower a few times, to help raise money for the United Way. Walking on an incline was normal for me because of the hills that I climbed as a child.

Further down the hill, we headed to the government offices, where I planned to request documents for my uncle. As we passed people, they greeted us, as if they knew us—it's the Montserrat way, and other islands have similar customs. At one point, my daughter was distracted and unintentionally passed a woman without saying hello. As the woman got closer to me, I said hello but she was already complaining. "How she pass me and no say good afternoon?" My daughter heard her and quickly corrected her mistake.

It wasn't 3:00 p.m. yet, so we had a lot of time to get to the government offices; we were told that they closed at 5:00 p.m. Walk there with me and you'll see that when we arrived, the door was locked. No one seemed to be inside.

"Maybe, they've all gone for a break," I thought.

After peering inside a few times and waiting for a few minutes, we checked with the police at the station nearby.

"Hello, officer."

"Good afternoon."

"No one seems to be at the offices next door. Do you know when they'll be back?"

"Well, it's Christmas time you know, so they went home because they didn't have any customers."

"Oh, I see," I said, a bit surprised and disappointed.

If I didn't know that I was home before, I knew then. Agility was going to be key on our visit. But it couldn't be compared to the agility that Montserratians have had to embrace while living with an active volcano.

We'd planned to visit the Montserrat Volcano Observatory and confirmed with the officer that we could get a bus nearby. The volcano had attracted experts from "away"—UK, US, other countries, and Caribbean islands. It had also attracted local experts, some of whom were born around the time that the volcano first erupted. We wanted to learn about how they monitor it and communicate their findings and advice.

As we waited for a bus, we heard honking and looked up to see my brother driving toward us. I'd promised to call him but hadn't done so yet.

"How did you find us?" I asked, amazed, although I shouldn't have been, given how I found him on our first day.

"Well, I went to the hotel and asked them if they knew where my sister was, and they told me that you came up here to run errands."

This was further confirmation that I was home.

"Is there no privacy on this island?" I joked.

"How you mean?" he said, chuckling. "This is Mon'srat!"

And, indeed, it was. Everybody knew everybody's business.

That was also how things were when I was a child. It might be one of the reasons that there was a near 0% violent crime rate. It's hard to commit a crime without everybody knowing about it, unless you are devious enough to hide in plain sight, as some rats did when I was a child.

Based on posters that we saw, there was more acknowledgement of peadophilia and efforts to address it. I don't think my four+ experiences were anomalous in my small village, and I've heard of other people's experiences; news reports often confirm similar statistics in other places across the world. Looking back, I would have liked to have seen a multi-pronged strategy—education, better laws, consistent enforcement, data collection of crimes, measurement of efforts to address and prevent them; health care education for parents/caregivers like my grandmother about how to protect their children from abuse, and the signs of abuse; education for teachers on the same; education for children on peadophilia, and empowerment to communicate about suspicious and actual abuse. Digital literacy should be part of a modern strategy…education about valuing women and children…about loving your neighbour as yourself…about advocacy and allyship. Public naming of paedophiles, as well as medical treatment/therapy for abused children, to help address physical and mental health. Abusers likely also need therapy but not at the expense of accountability.

As for the rats I encountered, most are likely dead. I don't hold any grudges or bitterness, so I won't use the "I forgive them" strategy. I also don't hold feelings of revenge, so I won't evoke the obeah practises of my ancestors, although it's tempting. Everyone experiences the ramifications of their actions, one way or another, though. That's just how the universe rolls.

Back to the Montserrat Volcano Observatory. We rolled up just as they were about to close. My brother knew the staff so he called out to them:

"Eh, my sister's here! Y'all show her around."

They were accommodating and informative. For the first time since arriving, we had a great view of the majestic volcano from outside and inside the Observatory. We learned about the tools that the experts use to monitor it, visually. They also monitor it for earthquakes, gases and other activities and regularly communicate their findings. They told us about going to places like Spanish Point and Farrels via helicopter to map material from eruptions, collect samples, conduct temperature checks, and more; it seemed like a dangerous job. I asked them about Harris.

"I heard that professional hikers, with guidance from volcano experts, take people on tours to Harris," I said.

"I strongly advise you not to go to Harris," one of them admonished me.

"Oh?"

"There's a chance that the volcano could erupt, without warning, and you can't outrun an eruption."

His words pierced and deflated my plan, leaving me with a tremendous feeling of disappointment. I wanted to go to Harris so badly. I would have hiked up that path that I imagined so clearly, all the way up to Barkin, then up to Cross Road, then up to Lookout, past the ruins of the Seventh Day Adventist Church, down past what remained of Mrs. Ponde's house, and down to my house to see what remained of it—what wild bushes and animals had moved in; what volcanic ashes and rocks had adorned it. But outrunning an erupting volcano was definitely not on my to-do list. *No sah!* Sadly, visiting my first home in Harris wasn't to be, at least not on this visit.

27

Finding Hope in the Ashes

In 2016, while I was in Montserrat, the premier was the Honourable Donaldson Romeo. He was elected in 2014 and during that election, candidates campaigned to a single constituency; Montserrat had seven before the volcano erupted. Candidates used social media to communicate their messages and a couple of them indicated they were from Harris. *They must be people that I know, or my mother knows—my peeps*, I thought.

As it turned out, one of them lived near the market; My mother knew his family well. The other one was my childhood neighbour—Miss Daisy's daughter. She was now Nurse Brenda, to use typical Montserratian honorifics. I learned more about what they and others had endured, and how they were forging on.

Imagine that you're driving with me through the new village called Lookout where Nurse Brenda and her brother took us.

It's where the government of Montserrat built houses for many who were displaced. We were on our way to Jack Boy Hill, on the northeast side. Arriving there, we could see the volcano very well. It was a similar vantage point as I would have had from my house, as a child; my village seemed so close.

"If I could push the hills blocking our view a little to the right, we could probably see Harris Lookout," I said to Nurse Brenda.

"Yes."

"We could probably also see what remains of my uncle's house and others. We might even see the Seventh Day Adventist church that I visited as a child. But the airport is gone!" I continued.

We could see the new land that the lava and pyroclastic flows had created—the volcano extended the island; the airport was in its path and paid the price. The cost for real estate is usually quite high, even the cost associated with creating land. The entire structure and all the energies of people and planes coming from and going "away" were buried.

"Yes, the airport is completely buried."

An archaeological site in the area where the Montserrat National Trust was supervising a dig was also buried, as well as villages like Trants and Spanish Point.

In the eerie stillness, the waves continued to swoop in and out, as if inviting the volcano to touch them again, with its blanket of lava, ashes and rock. A portion of a sugar mill nearby had survived the burial, though. It stood defiantly, offering a glimmer of hope.

• • •

Hope lingered in the air when we visited the Vue Pointe Hotel, where my uncle used to work. Continue to drive with me as we head there with Nurse Brenda. We could see that the beautiful houses nearby were spared. At the front of the hotel, the grounds were well-manicured. They contrasted with the slight discolouration on the roofs of some of the cottages on the property. It was from traces of volcanic ashes that once gently covered them like old, warm blankets. No one was outside, but we knew that the owners were working on opening conference rooms and preparing to host a New Year's Eve party; they had received funds from the government to clean up and renovate and had made a lot of progress.

We walked past the pool, which must have been touched by ashes from the volcano at one point; the unwelcomed deposits had long been removed.

"It's so blue and inviting!" I commented.

As we continued our tour, we could also see where the nearby Belham River Valley golf course was located—directly in the path of the volcano's lahar/mud flows, so it, too, was destroyed and buried.

Looking out from the Vue Pointe Hotel, we could see the volcano so clearly. I admired it, as I reminisced about the time when my uncle took my aunt/sister and I to the hotel. I remembered when I couldn't stop touching the bed sheets, towels, and other things; I'd never seen anything like them. This time, I was more disciplined and respectful and didn't touch anything. Hopefully, I set an example for the majestic volcano.

• • •

I remembered a neighbour in Harris who was an example of kindness—Mrs. Ponde. She was a pillar in our village. It was to her house that I went for ice many times. I'd seen her pictures on social media and was amazed that she was still alive, at 108! Later, I had the privilege of visiting her and her daughters, thanks to Nurse Brenda. Mrs. Ponde still looked about the same as she did when I was a child. She wasn't very talkative, but she seemed to remember me and enjoyed our company. I was grateful that we connected with her, as she would pass away a few months later.

• • •

I was disappointed that I couldn't connect with my father. He'd moved to Saint Kitts/Nevis shortly after the volcano erupted; I could see Nevis from our hotel, another "so close, but so far" place and moment.

A ferry provided services between the islands but stopped for the holidays, before we arrived. We would have to plan a Saint Kitts/Nevis trip another time, but, in the meantime, I spoke with my father by telephone.

"Hello, dad," I said mischievously, purposefully not identifying myself.

"Hello!" he replied in his usual cheerful way.

It was great to hear his voice, but I knew that he didn't know it was me. I asked which of his children he thought he was speaking with, and he started calling out names.

"Dad—dad!" I interrupted. "Let me give you a clue because your list of children is very long. We could be here all day."

Chuckle.

He'd told me that he had 18 children, but my brother thought there might be more; I know of twelve siblings but have only met five of them in person and three online.

I jokingly say sometimes that my father was very generous. He eventually settled into a stable, long-term marriage, but I don't know how he kept track of his 18 plus children. To help him figure out to which of his children he was speaking, I gave him the clue of my mother's name.

"Jacqueline! Jacqueline!" he said, even more cheerful.

"Oh, it's so good to hear your voice."

We chatted for a while, and then my children chatted with

him. I wished that we had spoken in person but was grateful that we at least connected by phone.

• • •

There were no phones ringing at the Montserrat Springs hotel, in Richmond Hill, though. It is where we went with my brother on another day. I don't remember visiting this area when I was a child, but it was sad to see that the volcano had destroyed it. From our hilltop view, look out far and wide at the ruins, with me, as far as your eyes can see.

There was Sturge Park, where I performed as a child. I saw a small part of its structure, still standing. There were Plymouth buildings and homes, but I couldn't see the Plymouth Public Market that I visited with my grandmother, nor the prison where my granduncle was a warden.

I was glad to see that the Plymouth Jetty was still there, although damaged. When I was a child, I remember seeing ships at the Jetty (this would have been the old one that Hurricane Hugo damaged). One year, a big ship from Guadeloupe was docked a short distance away. We took a small boat to it, for a school trip. There were a lot of men from Guadeloupe on the ship, in sailor's uniforms, and they seemed to like our teacher.

But we didn't see a single person or animal as we continued to look out at the devastation of our once beautiful town of Plymouth. In some cases, the lava buried or almost completely buried buildings, so only the roofs were visible. Some have called it the modern-day Pompeii—the buried city.

"Can you tell where the Glendon Hospital was?" my brother asked.

"No. Where was it?"

He pointed to where it would have been. Hurricane Hugo had destroyed it and the government rebuilt it, only to see it destroyed again by the volcano. They've since established a temporary hospital in St. John's and have plans to build a new one. I heard some people say, "We've been waiting so long for a new hospital!" In fact, they've been waiting for more than 26 years! That is a long time, over which each change in government seemed to delay things. But the current government, under the leadership of Honourable Joseph Easton Taylor-Farrell, is finally making progress, building on the work done by previous governments. Hopefully, there will be an improvement to services so that people like my grandmother, who had to travel to England for cancer treatment, will have access to specialized staff and services, where possible.

I used to listen to my grandmother praying for people who were in the hospital. She also prayed for her children in England and Canada, other relatives, friends, shut-ins, and prisoners. She usually ended her prayer in the same way.

"...And Lord, bless those in the lunatic asylum...Amen."

The volcano was comparable to the inmates running the asylum, per a book, by Alan Cooper, that I read in Computer Science—technical experts who create computer software are inappropriately in charge of design, sometimes. But the volcano may very well be appropriately in charge, given how Montserrat was created. It was redesigning parts of the island while highlighting the fragile concept of land ownership and control, and perhaps our changing climate. It's a good thing Montserratians know how to adapt and use unfortunate circumstances to their benefit.

I learned that businesses in Montserrat are profiting from the lava, boulders, and other volcanic material. When they eventually break down on the beaches and other areas (Fox's Bay, Belham Valley, Fort Ghaut, etc.), they mine and export the sand. It was great to see them in action. Sand mining is not without controversy, though. Understandably, some are concerned about noises and disturbances from trucks, as well as impact to nearby properties. They are also concerned about the environment—how mining sand might damage the land and impact turtles and other animals, highlighting once again the tense dynamics between capitalistic endeavours and environmental considerations. I'm optimistic that the government and businesses will figure out how to balance the various needs for economic growth and climate change management.

As part of a broader energy strategy (wind, solar, geothermal), Montserrat's government is leveraging the volcano and Montserrat's location to transition to environmentally friendly, green energy solutions—like using geothermal energy for electricity. They're drilling geothermal wells to access the heat from deep within the earth. Building productive wells is expensive, though, and some people have "let sleeping dogs lie" superstitions about digging near volcanos—an analogy that isn't lost on me. It will take time to transition, and the government will have to make bold energy transformation decisions while managing concerns and costs.

The volcano is also drawing tourists back to Montserrat. It was nice to see two cruise ships docked near the Little Bay port; once the in-flight port development project is complete, cruise ships will be able to dock at the port. It was also nice to learn that Montserratians and others were writing books and documentaries about the volcano. I'd love to see more children's books and also documentaries, television shows, and films showcasing our culture and history, telling our stories.

I also learned and saw that some who left Montserrat had returned and some from "away" were coming, too—from islands like Jamaica, South Asia, Haiti, Guyana, and other places. They are bringing their cultures; some Montserratians are concerned that Montserrat's culture might be changing. But our culture is already a mixture—West African and European customs, that we can clearly distinguish; it's possible that all cultures are Creole. Given the dynamic nature of culture, and the inevitability of immigration, Montserrat's culture will continue to evolve, and will continue to be part of its sustainable development. There are multicultural communities like Toronto, with many distinct cultures that we've come to appreciate and celebrate, even while working through challenges (xenophobia, etc.). Similarly, in a multicultural Montserrat, we can maintain our customs like Masquerades, goat water, saltfish, Johnny cakes, etc., while embracing and integrating others; sometimes, I might want to add a little ackee to my saltish.

Pre-volcano eruption, the economy was thriving and Montserrat was moving closer towards realizing independence from the UK; post-volcano eruption, we have some ground to make up and some are frustrated by the setback. Still, Montserrat had a middle- to upper-class feel. This gave me great comfort because I remember how poor we were when I was a child. People seemed to be thriving, despite the devastation. They were fighting for control of the asylum, if you will. While the Soufrière Hills volcano wreaked havoc on our beautiful island, and while there were still many challenges to work through (strengthening the private sector, addressing poverty for a proportion of the population, improving healthcare services, etc.), there were also positive impacts, some of which could help Montserrat become more confident with pursuing independence from the UK—which provides most of Montserrat's yearly operating budget—and maybe even become a leader on climate change initiatives.

Still, it behooves the bigger, richer countries to do their part; the efforts of small or developing countries won't matter if the biggest polluters don't hasten efforts to honour their commitments to reduce greenhouse gas emissions and limit global warming; in fact, the poor or developing countries will feel the biggest impacts if targets aren't met. Prime minister of Barbados, the Honourable Mia Motley, spoke powerfully to other world leaders at the 2021 United Nations Climate Change Conference (COP26), as well as to the media, about gaps in delivering on the Paris Agreement, vulnerabilities faced by small island developing states and other countries, how climate change is already impacting them (droughts, floods, disappearing marine life and coral reefs, extreme weather, sargassum seaweed), and how they need more climate finance. She urged leaders to "try harder." At the start of the Industrial Revolution, Indigenous voices were drowned out by the noise of progress; those voices are now being amplified—it's near impossible to avoid hearing them in our digital age. We already know how to radically revolutionize our world to gain efficiencies; we also know how to focus our priorities (e.g., addressing existential threats like a pandemic). That same innovative mindset, as well as our global interconnectedness, aided by traditional and modern technologies, can help us realize a climate revolution. We and our descendants should only have to live with Elon Musk, Jeff Bezos, Sir Richard Branson, and others, on an inhospitable planet like Mars, if we choose to, not because we have to because we destroyed our only home.

• • •

From our safe vantage point in Richmond Hill, we continued to take in the incredible changes to the area. We had a clear view of the volcano's southern side from which it would have rained lahar and pyroclastic flows indiscriminately on Plymouth. It was an awesome sight to behold—so high and mighty, so intimidating, so quiet but powerful. It rested peacefully and gently blew steam into the air—an active, complex system with its own weather, as we learned from the volcano experts. The earth's tectonic plates recycle into molten/liquid rock (magma), then push up through the surface to form domes that eventually collapse, spewing lava, rocks, gases, and ashes.

Similar to what we saw on the other side of the island, the

volcano buried just about everything in its way. It carved out Grand Canyon-like grooves, scorched trees and bushes; but in some areas, it created the perfect conditions for them to spring up again, given the rich volcanic soil. They grew wildly on its sides in green splendour. They covered Sturge Park and parts of Plymouth. Even in and around the destroyed Montserrat Springs Hotel, ferns, likely some kusha bushes, and other trees were flourishing. It was as if they were rising out of death and destruction; they, too, were fighting for control of the asylum.

Time will tell whether the volcano will knock them down again with another eruption. Time will also determine the number of rounds before they, and ultimately Montserratians, are once again in control of the whole island, if only for another 400 years, before the fight begins again. Hopefully, the fight isn't more frequent as a result of climate change.

28

My Open Circle

One day, we'd stopped at Runaway Ghaut, in Woodlands, north of Salem, on the west side of the island. It's where water streams down from the Centre Hills mountains enroute to the sea. A sign there reads:

"If you drink from this burn, to Montserrat you will return."

It's based on the fact that the French attacked Montserrat in the 1700s (possibly also in the 1600s). Then the English drove them out, as they escaped via Runaway Ghaut. The French returned to occupy Montserrat multiple times but ultimately, it was returned to Britain. Like the French, my daughter and other visitors will be back, having sealed their "return to Montserrat contract" with a drink of Runaway Ghaut water (which Montserratians will tell you is one of the best sources in the Caribbean, if not the world).

And also like the French, there are lessons that we all have to learn, sometimes after multiple experiences.

For me, one of those lessons is to not take things or people for granted. It's so easy to do, repeatedly. When Montserrat was thrusted into the news cycle, I learned more about the history of the Soufrière Hills, as well as how broader global changes can potentially shift natural cycles; I learned more about Montserrat's natural and socio-political transformations which have present-day and generational impacts. It felt like I, too, experienced a transformation, a deeper connection to my culture and a stronger need to preserve and share it. I'm more acutely aware of its fragility (our fragility), in light of natural disasters (volcano eruptions, hurricanes, earthquakes) and existential threats (pandemics, climate change, etc.). I also feel more connected to my ancestors through customs like the Masquerade dance, but I know that I'll need to do my part to carry on their (our) legacy, by helping to protect our bigger home.

When I returned from Montserrat, I made sure to reconnect with my paternal grandmother and family, who live in Canada. I'd lost contact with them over the years, but learning more about my roots also reminded me of the many branches (present and past) that make me who I am. So we visited them later and my children met them for the first time. We shared pictures and stories from our visit to Montserrat with them and had a great visit. I also shared pictures and stories with my colleagues at work.

• • •

Imagine that you're with me at work. Of course, work is intrinsically hard, but trust me that this won't be painful. Walk with me as I go to the technical support area for help with an application. As I hand over my laptop, I ask my co-worker Gerry if he likes my background—a picture from my visit to Montserrat. I anticipate an interesting conversation about it—the same anticipation I felt when people I met at school, work, church, social events and while travelling within and outside Canada, asked me: "Where are you from?"

They probably heard my strong Montserratian accent when I first immigrated to Canada and the way I still say certain words. It's not lost on me that some ask the question in a way that can be perceived as invalidating, because it implies you don't belong in the place that you call home. I didn't experience that, but I know many have. When people asked me where I'm from, I took the opportunity to tell them about Montserrat, while showing that it's okay to be different and help rephrase the "alien in your own land" narrative. Navigating these interactions might be easier for first-generation citizens like me, than for subsequent generations, though; we're from somewhere else and are connected to both our birth home and new home.

"I'm originally from Montserrat!" I'd proudly say. In return, I'd get a few common responses.

"Montserrat? Where's that?"

"Oh…is that the place with the active volcano? Does the island still exist? Isn't it completely destroyed?"

"Montserrat near Barcelona, Spain?"

Those who lived in, or immigrated from larger islands like Jamaica, would sometimes remark:

"Oh…small island people!"

Some people who knew about Antigua and learned that Montserrat is near it have said,

"I've been to Antigua, but I've never heard of Montserrat!"

As I spoke with my co-worker, I wondered which one of the common responses about Montserrat I'd hear. Then I surprisingly heard him say,

"Oh! Montserrat? My father-in-law's from Montserrat."

"What!?"

He told me his father-in-law's name—I didn't recognize it. But Montserrat is so small that the high likelihood of my mother knowing him or his family made me want to jump up and down right there in the office. I didn't. But I did check with my mother later.

"Mom, my colleague's father-in-law is from Montserrat."

She listened as I shared the information about him.

"Do you know him?"

"Yes, of course," she said. "He's our neighbour, Brother Reiny's son."

This was the same Brother Reiny who lived near the Black Mango tree in Harris, who told me "Next time, don't run" when his dog bit me. I was used to Reiny, his first name, and didn't connect his son's last name to him. I also didn't have any memories of his son—he immigrated to Canada before I was born and had a daughter named Sharon, who married my co-worker. Sharon may have even seen me when she visited Montserrat, in the early 1970s.

After being away from Montserrat for so long, I couldn't make a full circle return to my village. I couldn't walk past Brother Reiny's house to get to my house, or eat mangoes that had fallen from the nearby Black Mango tree. I couldn't go to the airport from which I left the island, or create my own path, north of the airport, to hike to my house. Taking a taxi to Harris as I drove past nearby villages was out of the question. So was going to Plymouth, walking its streets and visiting the Plymouth Market, Plymouth Prison, or the Glendon hospital. Many of the old footprints, handprints, structures, fixtures, and remains of the deceased (recent and ancient) have been entombed and will be the delight of archaeologists. They're already documenting things and will continue well into the future to carefully dig, collect, and curate artifacts of villages, Town, and other areas long buried. And I'm sure that they'll have to sort out conflicts with regards to protecting historical sites.

I don't know if Harris, Plymouth, or any of the other impacted areas will ever be redeveloped; most will never be the same. But like those who've already visited their homes, I know that one day, when it's safe, I, too, will explore what remains of my village—perhaps with cutlass in hand, clearing kusha and other bushes. I'm not sure what I'll do if I see a snake, though. But it is there that I'll face the lofty giant, from the same vantage point that I had from my home in Harris. It is there that I'll stand tall despite nagging fears. I'll feel relieved and surprised as the volcano retreats back into a deep sleep. And it won't be a dream, but rather a quiet reflection—a meditation about a battle long fought in Montserrat, by people both near and far away; people and places that are connected in sometimes unexpected ways. I'll be reminded that when I look back at where I'm from, to not only wave goodbye, but wave hello more often and take the time to appreciate the beauty of home. I most certainly don't want to ever ***have to*** do this kind of reflecting from Mars!

Looking down at Little Bay, from Brades.

Viewing Little Bay from Tropical Mansions Suite,
and two ships docked off the Little Bay port.

Here we see the Public Market in the foreground and the Cultural Centre in the background, and no traffic!

In Montserrat, many places are either up or down a steep hill. In this picture, my daughter thinks that I, a Montserratian, was struggling to walk up Brades Road.

My daughter walking down Brades Road, not struggling at all.

My son, daughter and my brother, Silford, observing the volcano, from the Montserrat Volcano Observatory.

Here is my brother, Silford.

My daughter and son on the balcony at Tropical Mansions Suites, with Little Bay in the backdrop.

Me and my daughter in front of Vue Pointe Hotel. The majestic Soufrière Hills volcano is in the backdrop.

Viewing the volcano and the devastation in Plymouth.

Viewing the destroyed Montserrat Springs Hotel.

This is also part of the Montserrat Springs Hotel.

Viewing the devastation of Plymouth, with buildings and landscape taken over by flourishing trees and vegetation.

Viewing the devastation in Plymouth.

Viewing the devastation of Sturge Park.
A small part of the Sturge Park structure stands defiantly, on the left.

Viewing the damage to the Plymouth jetty.

Viewing the volcano from the east of the island.
Harris is behind the mountain in the foreground.

Viewing the devastation of the W.H. Bramble
Airport. It is completely buried.

Masquerades, the mesmerizing visual storytellers,
taking the stage, at the Cultural Centre.

It was a sad time for me when my father died in September 2021, after being ill for a few months. I am grateful to have spoken with him a few times before he passed. He was a kind and loving father. This picture was taken in 2020, on my father's 80th birthday. R.I.P. dad (1940 to 2021)

Epilogue

Look back at Earth, our home, from the edge of space, with me. We'll see her surrounded by the atmosphere—multiple layers of gas that look blue and fragile, juxtaposed against the darkness of space. Her powerful, natural processes and cycles are constantly at work, but sometimes she's sending signals about things gone, or going wrong—clues about her state, like warning and error messages sent from a computer or tell-tale markers from a diagnostic image. Whether you think she started with a bang or a hand, there's no disputing the power, wonder, and awe that she evokes. She has her own Masquerade dance, if you will, a colourful blend of all the cultures and peoples that have called her home, connecting us all in profound ways.

Like Montserrat's Masquerades and those of other countries, we do well to invest in her maintenance and protection and pay keen attention to her movements, whether atmospheric, surface, oceanic, tectonic, or other. After seeing her display of power on the Soufrière Hills, I've never looked at a mountain the same way again; I can't and won't pass them like pictures on a wall. I imagine what's underneath—what shifts are in progress, what plates are clanking and colliding, what forces are at work…if I only pay attention to what I can see, I might end up thousands of feet beneath her surface, in the bowels of an ocean liner, or under hundreds of feet of material expelled from her innermost parts.

Similarly, when life throws challenges our way that feel like non-stop volcanic eruptions, if we only pay attention to the results or manifestation (the pyroclastic flows devouring everything that we've built), we'll ignore the root causes, at our peril. While we may have to move out of the way and rebuild elsewhere, it behooves us to look back, do some analysis and determine what we can do differently to get a different outcome, where possible; a good way to learn and grow and avoid repeating ill-fated decisions.

Growing up in Montserrat had a huge impact on who I am—my personal identity. And immigrating to Canada further shaped me, and, of course, so does my ongoing life experiences. In Montserrat, we had few material possessions, and even when we finally got electricity, we didn't get a fridge, stove, television, telephone, or anything powered by electricity. We were poor.

Yet, having few material possessions helped me appreciate the simple things, and my culture: the sweet taste of grafted July mangoes that I could pick off the tree in our yard and sink my teeth into, as its juices filled my mouth and escaped down my chin neck and fingers…playing marbles, hopscotch, jump rope, jacks and other games… makeshift concerts, celebrations and Festivals… mouth-watering goat water, cassava bread, Miss BeeBee's bread, Johnny cakes and more…regularly attending church...jumbie rituals and stories…walking up and down hills, going to rivers and "bush"... running errands for my grandmother…speaking patois (Montserrat Creole)...visiting other villages. These experiences are part of my cultural identity, as are the places that I've lived in

Canada. I have all of my experiences stored in my memory bank and feel happiness and joy when I tap into them.

My grandmother had a theory about happiness, if you remember—that skinny people aren't happy. Generalizations/stereotypes don't account for differences, of course. It's possible that some people, like me, are naturally skinny, regardless of how we feel. Generalizations aside, I've had some gut wrenching, painful experiences that would threaten anyone's happiness. In any community, you will find good and unwelcome creatures, and that was certainly the case in both Montserrat and Canada—there are rats everywhere in the world, and I've encountered a few of the human and non-human kind. I've also encountered well-intended disciplinarians and some that just seemed to want others to feel the pain and misery they themselves experienced from their own tortured existence.

Thankfully, I wasn't a miserable child growing up in Montserrat, despite the negative experiences that dotted my childhood. They were outnumbered by the bigger dots of my many positive experiences, and a couple that were major like meeting my father when I was eight years old, and, after many years of dreaming about going "away" to see my mother, how I finally did, and met her when I was ten years old. I don't think that I thought that seeing my mother would make me happier; it's natural to want to be with your parents, or at least know who they are. But once I immigrated to Canada, it didn't take long for me to start planning to leave home at a young age. I didn't like my stepfather, nor did he like me, and the situation became volatile enough I felt something really bad was likely to happen. This experience further shaped who I am by forcing me to advocate for myself.

Looking back, I can see that moving from one country to another or from one home to another or from one relationship to another doesn't bring happiness or joy. Joy and happiness are within and based on how I interpret the world. If I stop to think about how much I appreciate eating a July mango and the wonder of genetic engineering or the fact that my ancestors used creativity to manage their suffering, like creating the Masquerade dance, the original form of calypso, blending cultures to create their own cultural identity, it gives me a feeling of contentment and peace; I feel joy and I take it wherever I go. It doesn't mean that I will stay in a bad situation or tolerate abuse. You have to recognize when your ratio of negative to positive experiences is increasing unreasonably and when it's time to do something, walk or run away. Sometimes it's best to run! This is what I teach my children.

When they were teenagers, they used to complain about not being allowed to sleep at their friends' homes. So, I finally told them about my childhood experiences. I didn't want them to experience the same things; I was fiercely protective, or they'd say over-protective. This was on full display when their father was delayed at work one day and asked his friend to pick them up from my house—we were separated/divorced at the time. I interrogated their father about who the person was and he insisted that he knew him well, that he was a good person. I couldn't be sure so I said hello to the friend, then told him point blank,

"If you touch my children, I'll kill you."

Of course, it was an exaggerated way (maybe) of telling him that I had my eyes on him and that he'd be held accountable if he hurt my children. Thankfully, I didn't have to kill anyone, and end up living the prison life that my grand uncle, warden of Montserrat's Plymouth Prison, was likely trying to help me avoid.

I left Montserrat in 1977. Before I returned there for the first time in 2016, I'd reconnected with my childhood neighbour, Nurse Brenda. As we chatted, I started giving her an imaginary tour of my village, as I remembered it. She was amazed at how much I remembered even though I hadn't been back in decades. This is because Montserrat (home) is in my heart and memory and will always be there. Even my great memories from experiences in the areas the volcano destroyed will continue to be stored there; they'll continue to be part of my sense of joy, although I still feel sad sometimes when I see pictures of the devastation—I still grieve the loss. I'm optimistic that we can take care of the Earth and minimize this kind of devastation and grief.

Jacqueline Greer Graham. November 2021.
Photo by Trinity Design

Jacquelinegreergraham.com
Instagram: https://www.instagram.com/jacquelinegreergraham/
Twitter: https://twitter.com/jacquelinegrgr

About the Author

Jacqueline Greer Graham is a Canadian citizen who was born in Montserrat, British West Indies. While working from home as a manager in the health information technology space, during the corona virus global pandemic, she was inspired to write this book. The pandemic highlighted for her how quickly life can change, and even end, and how important it is to capture her rich experiences for the benefit of her children, and others.

Jacqueline is excited about sharing her story and holds the opinion that you should write/record/share yours, too, even if you don't publish it; it's an enlightening and therapeutic experience from which others can also benefit. She would love to read and learn from her fore parents' memoirs, if only they existed.

Jacqueline lives in Ontario, Canada, and has two children—Gabrielle and Lemuel.

Manufactured by Amazon.ca
Bolton, ON